Korean–American Relations

Korean-American Relations

DOCUMENTS PERTAINING TO THE
FAR EASTERN DIPLOMACY
OF THE UNITED STATES

VOLUME I

THE INITIAL PERIOD, 1883–1886

Edited, with an Introduction, by
GEORGE M. McCUNE AND JOHN A. HARRISON

Berkeley and Los Angeles · 1951
UNIVERSITY OF CALIFORNIA PRESS

UNIVERSITY OF CALIFORNIA PRESS
BERKELEY AND LOS ANGELES
CALIFORNIA

CAMBRIDGE UNIVERSITY PRESS
LONDON, ENGLAND

COPYRIGHT, 1951, BY THE
REGENTS OF THE UNIVERSITY OF CALIFORNIA

To E.B.M.

Preface

THIS IS THE first volume of a projected three-volume series on Korean-American relations from 1883 to 1905. The first United States representative to Korea arrived in Seoul in 1883. In 1905 Korea lost control of her foreign affairs to Japan and the United States withdrew its Legation from Korea. During the intervening twenty-two years the United States Legation in Seoul, as the only "neutral" in the international struggle for control of Korea, enjoyed the confidence of the King of Korea and the Korean Foreign Office and, at times, the esteem of the other nations involved in this struggle. A great deal of this is recorded in the archives of the United States Legation at Seoul. In addition, the American representatives were, generally speaking, able men committed to their basic instructions to work for the integrity of the Korean Kingdom, and their dispatches and memoranda render an excellent picture of the late nineteenth- and early twentieth-century contest for hegemony over Northeast Asia among China, Japan, Russia, and England in which Korea was the pivot and eventual victim.

The record of Western diplomacy in East Asia has been imperfectly told, partly because the modern history of East Asia is imperfectly known. This is understandable because of the language barriers and the difficulty of access to the records. But throughout the record which does exist there runs, as an amazing leitmotif, an almost continuous denigration of the role of American diplomacy and American diplomatists. It is hoped that this small series will help to make more clear the processes of American diplomacy and the record of American representatives in East Asia.

The selection of documents for this volume was based upon the principle that nothing essential to an understanding of the American role in Korea should be omitted, within the limits of the space available for publication. The most pertinent and meaningful dispatches have been included; more routine messages or messages that have found publication in some other form have been left out. The documents have been arranged under four general categories, three of which correspond to the most important questions facing Korea from 1883 to 1887; the fourth deals with the activities and personnel of the United States Legation in Seoul.

The documents are cited verbatim. This means that some fantastic inconsistencies in spelling, capitalization, punctuation, and grammar have been preserved. Some examples may be cited; within one dispatch Yuan Shih K'ai is referred to as *Yuan, Yuen, Youen* and *Yuen Si Kwai*. Acting Chargé George Foulk spells his name *Foulk,* but Minister Foote writes of him as *Foulke*. Sir Robert *Hart* is called Sir Robert *Heart*. The capital city of Korea is spelled variously, *Seoul, Soul, Söul* and *Soel*. Many words are misspelled. Quite often a standard prefix is followed by a hyphen as in *re-iterate*. *Tientsin* is spelled as *Tiensin* and *Tien-Tsin* to mention a few of the variations. It is felt that nothing would be gained by attempting to make corrections so numerous as to change the tenor and, in some cases, the intent of the dispatches. In a very few cases a fragmentary message has been included because of its importance although, owing to the condition of the original archives from which they were taken, only a part was legible. To save space and permit of printing more material the lengthy and standard Victorian salutations and endings have been deleted, the message being introduced with its number, date and place of origin, the title of the addressee, and being closed with the name of the originator.

It is hoped by the editors that this compilation may prove of interest to the laymen and of use to the scholar and that it may serve as a springboard for other students interested in uncovering the little-known and badly told history of the United States in Eastern Asia.

The editors wish to take this opportunity to thank Professor John D. Hicks of the University of California, Berkeley, for his constant help and encouragement.

University of California, Berkeley   G.M.M.
University of Florida, Gainesville   J.A.H.

Contents

	INTRODUCTION	1
1.	THE UNITED STATES LEGATION IN SEOUL	23
2.	SECURING AMERICAN ADVISERS FOR THE KOREAN GOVERNMENT	53
3.	ENGLAND, RUSSIA, AND KOREA	69
4.	CHINA, JAPAN, AND THE STRUGGLE FOR CONTROL OF KOREA	95
	INDEX TO DOCUMENTS	159

Introduction

DURING THE international struggle for control of the Korean peninsula, which lasted through the last quarter of the nineteenth century and the first decade of the twentieth, the United States representative in Seoul was often regarded by the Korean authorities as the symbol of a beneficent power that would indisputably guarantee the integrity of the Korean nation. In reality the United States representative in Seoul was forced to play the role of hapless quartermaster, who is expected to bring the drifting vessel to safety minus accurate bearings or adequate motive power.

With the arrival of Lucius H. Foote as Envoy Extraordinary and Minister Plenipotentiary of the United States to Korea (1883) there was inaugurated the initial period of Korean-American relations, which was to last until the middle of 1887, at which time the Chinese Government asked that the former acting Chargé at Seoul, George C. Foulk, be recalled for having encouraged the Korean Government in a course of action independent of China. During this period the United States, through its representative at Seoul, was often the mediating party in a most complicated situation. The Japanese-Korean Treaty of 1876 had recognized Korea as an independent and sovereign nation. This had given impetus to the formation of a "progressive" group among Korean officials who, impatient of China and the Chinese system, were impressed by the technical and political advances made by Japan during the early Meiji period. The conservative opposition to this group was divided between the party of the highly nationalistic, reactionary and Confucianist ex-Regent and the equally reactionary but pro-Chinese party of the Queen of Korea. In 1882 the ex-Regent was seized by China and kept in seclusion in China.

This act removed the influence of the former Regent but the highly personal power politics of the Korean nobility abated not a whit. It is not possible, in a brief compass, to simplify the variable and complex internal political strife of the Korea of that day. But the shifting groups and ambitions so aligned themselves that, by the time of Foote's arrival there existed an undercover but nevertheless vicious struggle.

This involved conflict between the ex-Regent, the Min family (to which the Queen belonged), and the King. The King's and Queen's parties were in agreement about Westernization but opposed in policies toward China and Japan. The ex-Regent opposed all Westernization and thereby ran into trouble with the other groups. The year before the arrival of Foote the ex-Regent, goaded by the growing ascendancy at Seoul of Chinese and Japanese influence and by the Shufeldt treaty, had provoked a revolt against the Japanese in Seoul as well as against the King and Queen. Both China and Japan rushed troops into Korea. Trouble was averted when an indemnity and apology was proffered Japan and by the Chinese withdrawing and taking with them, into exile, the ex-Regent. By such compromises and maneuvers war between China and Japan was avoided but domestic Korean politics remained inflamed and ever threatened to become a *casus belli* between China and Japan. In addition to the domestic broil the opening of Korea was fast knotting a skein of conflicting interests among the Powers concerned in East Asia. China, not desirous of relinquishing her historical claims in and on Korea, was pressing these claims in inverse proportion to her ability to enforce them. Great Britain, fearful that an independent Korea would weaken the Chinese barrier to Russian expansion southward, set herself to stiffen Chinese claims to hegemony over Korea. Russia realized that Korea was the strategic key to the retention and exploitation of Eastern Siberia. Japan thought that Korea was not only the vital base to her continental expansion but also a shield against invasion. The United States, desiring peace and on friendly terms with all countries concerned, was to find that her legation in Seoul was the focal point for the domestic and international intrigue which the prospects of an independent Korea had set in motion. Taking the position that Korea was a sovereign and independent state the United States was to endeavor to maintain peace between the Powers and to make concrete the nebulous "independence" of Korea. Although generally speaking, the American representatives in Seoul were able men cognizant of the complexities of the situation and really devoted to establishing the autonomy of Korea, their efforts were to be in vain.

American statesmanship was neither ready nor able to effect a Far Eastern policy of moment. The American State Department in the post-Civil War period was at one of its low ebbs in ability and vision. The Congress was more than usually parsimonious in allotting sufficient funds to maintain a respectable Foreign Service and, all too often, the efforts of the men on the spot at Seoul were negated either by ineffective instructions or—far too often—no instructions at all. As the only party to the Korean struggle with disinterested authority the American effort could have been far less futile

Introduction

than it was. The following paragraphs are a chronological record of the initial period of that effort, synthesized from the archives of the American Legation at Seoul and the records of the Department of State.

When Minister Foote arrived at Seoul in May, 1883, the King of Korea "danced with joy."[1] The King and his adherents had viewed the Shufeldt treaty as a wedge to free Korea from Chinese domination. The revolt of July, 1882, had resulted, through troop movements led by Wu Ch'ang-Ching with Yuan Shih K'ai on his staff, in a renewed Chinese lien on Korea. Believing that this obvious control would result in an American disavowal of the Shufeldt treaty the King was discouraged. But the arrival of Foote and the exchange of ratifications on the treaty brought the King's "progressives" to such a point of hope that they set in motion a wholesale housecleaning of Chinese advisers. They were basing their hope and their housecleaning on the premise that the United States would furnish capable advisers for the Korean Foreign Office and Army.

Initial instructions to Foote were concerned with the concept of the independence of Korea and extension of trade rights to American citizens.[2]

The State Department was aware of the Chinese attitude toward Korea. From a translation of the trade regulations between Korea and China, Secretary of State Freylinghuysen inferred that the King of Korea had not "any independent control beyond the nomination of the negotiators who were practically controlled by the Chinese Superintendent of Northern Trade."[3] Furthermore, since this Superintendent of Northern Trade was to correspond on terms of equality with the King of Korea, "the broad fact remains that the King of Korea is treated not as a sovereign but as the equal only of a high but subordinate official of China."[4] However, the course of action for Foote was clearly defined. "As far as we are concerned Corea is an independent sovereign power."[5] And this is later reinforced in the same instructions; "You will remember that for all purposes of intercourse between the United States and Corea the King is a sovereign and that with sovereign states only do the United States treat."[6] Conversely Foote was to treat the Chinese agents in Korea as subordinate officials. Since these officials had only commercial duties, Foote was to hold no communication with them without applying to the State Department for instructions.

---

[1] Foulke to Secretary of the Navy, enclosure to No. 128, Foote to Freylinghuysen, December 17, 1884.
[2] No. 3, Freylinghuysen to Foote, March 17, 1883.
[3] Ibid. By the Chinese Superintendent of Northern Trade is meant Li Hung Chang.
[4] Ibid.
[5] Ibid.
[6] Ibid.

Foote was also to give his attention to the discriminatory trade regulations of 1882 between China and Korea. This pact forbid non-Chinese but permitted Chinese the following privileges:

1. To reside in and travel to and from specified points in the interior.
2. To travel in the interior under passport.
3. To transport native produce from one open port to another.
4. To bring native produce from the interior or to take it into the interior.
5. Equality in customs duties.

The United States could not consent to this practical monopoly of Korean trade by China.[7] However, no active remedial measures were to be taken for a time owing to the anti-Western feeling among certain groups in Korea.

With these two points in mind, Korea as a sovereign state and equality of trade, Foote proceeded to Yokohama where the Shufeldt treaty was being kept. In Yokohama he was instructed to discuss his mission with the experienced Bingham, American Minister to Japan, and then to proceed to Seoul. Since Korea was beyond existing Pacific area mail and cable communications, Foote was told to take advantage of any means, including the United States Asiatic Squadron, to maintain communication with the State Department.

In Tokyo by the end of April, 1883, Foote sought a conference with the Chinese representative there in order "to impress upon him the real attitude of the United States in regard to Korean affairs."[8] Foote took this step because there was no Chinese Imperial representative at Seoul and he desired to correct "certain adverse influence" that he thought might have been brought to bear on the Chinese Government.[9] At this time he was informed by Sir Harry Parkes, the British Minister to Japan, that the odds were against the Government of China favoring any treaties made by Korea. Parkes went further and told Foote that he (Parkes) was personally against the English-Korean treaty just concluded by Admiral Willis. Foote was drawn to the inference that Parkes' pessimism was mostly based on the apprehension that other Oriental nations would request modifications in their present treaties with England that would bring these treaties more in line with the Shufeldt treaty. At the conclusion of his stay in Japan Foote left for Chemulpo with the impression that "the Corean Government is not sufficiently strong either to control its own people or to resist outside pressure."[10]

---
[7] *Ibid.*
[8] No. 4, Foote to Freylinghuysen, May 1, 1883.
[9] *Ibid.*
[10] *Ibid.*

Introduction 5

Foote arrived in Seoul on May 12, 1883. His official family consisted of Mrs. Foote, C. S. Scudder, his private secretary, P. L. Jouey of the Smithsonian Institute, and Saito, his translator. Within two weeks of his arrival the opinions of Freylinghuysen and Parkes were confirmed by observation. He noted that the Korean Government "had little real strength," the country was "stagnant and impoverished" and, despite the many well-intentioned men in the country, years of subservience to "the dictation of China and Japan have created a degree of timidity."[11] His initial talk with the Chief of the Korean Foreign Office on the matter of trade regulations left him with the impression that "the Corean Government feels and fears the omnipresent espionage of China."[12] The delight of the King in having an American representative at the scene was evidenced in a letter of the King to President Arthur commending Foote as being "on excellent terms with us, honest and upright; and in the transaction of business at the capitol he is always in accord with the views of my government," and in a constant seeking of the advice of Foote on matters of administration.[13] This placed Foote in a delicate position and a lonely one. Both England and Germany had declined to ratify their treaties with Korea. Both countries felt that following ratification of the existing treaties China would demand modification of her pacts especially with respect to the traffic in opium and extrality. Foote had heard this from Bingham in Tokyo via the Department of State. Bingham added that the British had done their utmost to prevent ratification of the Shufeldt treaty.[14] The State Department approved of Foote's tendering advice to the King but added that such advice was "to be regarded as personal only when not expressly covered by instructions from here."[15] This was peculiar advice indeed, for seldom, if ever, in the critical years that followed, was the Department to issue instructions to Seoul that were of value or perception. The issues that were to face Foote and his successor Foulk; the reassertion of Chinese control over Korea, the widening Sino-Japanese rift, the slow Russian encroachment on the borders, the placing of strategic advisers with the Korean Government—all these affairs of state and the more mundane but equally important problem of rendering effective service to the United States without sufficient funds for a proper Legation residence

---

[11] No. 9, Foote to Freylinghuysen, May 26, 1883.

[12] No. 11, Foote to Freylinghuysen, June 30, 1883.

[13] No. 11, Davis to Foote, June 29, 1883, with enclosure 1688 (Bingham to Freylinghuysen, May 30, 1883).

[14] Note also, No. 4, Foote to Freylinghuysen, May 1, 1885, where Foote had been "credibly informed that under the direction of Sir Harry, an agent of the British Government has been in Corea for some months."

[15] No. 21, Freylinghuysen to Foote, September 18, 1883.

or even for salary or expenses—these issues were to be faced by the man on the spot dependent entirely on his own judgment and sources of information. Foote, and later Foulk, were to feel deserted by their own government at the end of an uncertain line of communications and Foote knew that, "every public act and word of mine is reported to the Chinese and Japanese Governments."[16] On the other hand it must be pointed out that the Department was aware of the obstacles of time and space. "I desire to say to you that the Department approves the discretion you evince in treating matters affecting the relations of China and Japan with Corea, to which, at this distance of time and place, much must be trusted."[17]

Foote relied on his Naval Aide, George C. Foulk, Ensign, USN, who spoke Korean and who, from 1884 to 1887 was the center of "progressivism" in Korea. With excellent sources of information he kept Foote abreast of the political situation and at the same time advised the King and his coterie. He warned Foote in October, 1884, that the political situation was such that it could only be resolved in blood—which it was the following month—and he was an acute political reporter.[18]

Foote soon discovered the great specific of Western diplomacy in the Orient. "The influence of foreigners holding confidential positions in these Oriental countries, seems to add largely to the influence of their respective governments."[19] The King of Korea had given Foote the unprecedented honor of an interview *à deux* in the private apartments of the King. Here he thanked Foote for the disinterested activities of the American Government and requested Foote's advice in negotiating new treaties with England and Germany. He then asked Foote for the services of an American who knew Chinese to whom he would give the second highest rank in the Korean Foreign Office and an American military man to whom he would give the second highest military rank in the Kingdom.[20] Foote requested the services of advisers and did what he could about the treaties. When, in October, 1883, Sir Harry Parkes and Herr Zappe arrived to resume treaty talks Parkes told Foote that the Korean Government was "moving too rapidly"—meaning within the orbit of the United States. Foote remained noncommittal but expressed the desire of the American Government to see Germany and England enter upon equitable treaty relations with Korea.[21]

[16] No. 12, Foote to Freylinghuysen, June 30, 1883.
[17] No. 17, Adee to Foote, August 17, 1883.
[18] See No. 128, Foote to Freylinghuysen, December 17, 1884—enclosure written by Foulk on the Korean political situation.
[19] No. 32, Foote to Freylinghuysen, October 19, 1883.
[20] *Ibid.*
[21] No. 37, Foote to Freylinghuysen, October 30, 1883.

Introduction 7

The remainder of 1883 and the first months of 1884 were quiet enough. In October, 1883, Foote had his first row with Herr Von Möllendorf, Adviser to the Korean Foreign Office. Von Möllendorf, a German placed in office by Li Hung Chang, was attempting to restrict all communication with the Korean Foreign Office to himself. He suggested to Foote that under the terms of the Shufeldt treaty the American representative in Seoul had no right, "to interpose objections or to make suggestions in regard to the General Trade Regulations which the Government of Corea proposes to decree."[22] Foote overrode this by stating bluntly that the treaty was ratified because the United States thought it would help Korea not that the United States cared for Korean commerce. Foote further stated that if this treaty were to prevent friendly intercourse between the two countries it were better torn up. The result, "was as I anticipated, that everything asked for was conceded without a dissenting word."[23] The remainder of the winter 1883–1884 was spent uneventfully. There was an exchange with the State Department on the matter of finances allotted Foote. His secretary was serving without salary, he had no money for clerk hire and none for the purchase of a suitable building and ground for a legation. The Department submitted an estimate to Congress calling for a rise in salary and additional expense money. Neither was granted.

Significantly enough the first important dispatch of Foote for 1884 relates to the question of advisers for the Korean Government. At a private audience the King asked whether the recent treaties with England and Germany could be modified before ratification. Advised against this by Foote he pressed for an answer to his request of six months previous for advisers in military and foreign affairs.[24] This was the second time within a month that Foote had been reminded of this request and in passing it along to the Department he pointed out that the United States had done this service for Japan and that he could not understand the silence upon this matter with respect to Korea.[25]

The Korean Mission to the United States returned in June, 1884, and Min Yong Ik, who had led the mission, said to Foote, "I was born in the dark, I went out into the light, and now I have returned into the dark again: I cannot yet see my way clearly but I hope to soon."[26] Foote named Min as the probable leader of the progressive group. This was a poor estimate, for

---
[22] No. 34, Foote to Freylinghuysen, October 23, 1883.
[23] *Ibid.*
[24] No. 66, Foote to Freylinghuysen, April 26, 1884.
[25] No. 62, Foote to Freylinghuysen, April 8, 1884.
[26] No. 83, Foote to Freylinghuysen, June 17, 1884.

Min was to become one of the leaders of the reactionary opposition in Korea completely under the thumb of the Chinese.

Western trade with Korea was "sluggish." Barter was the chief means of trade, there being only bulky copper cash for money, and the Chinese and Japanese were the only nations able to compete on this basis.[27] However, there were chances for improvement and Foote recommended consulates at Wonsan, Pusan, and Inchun. Foulk arrived in June, 1884. Land was selected for the site of an American consulate at Inchun but there was no money for purchase. This placed Foote in an embarrassing position, since other nations had already bought and paid for their sites. A charter for steamers operating on Korean rivers and coastal waters was granted to an American firm, Middleton and Co. of Yokohama. Another American company was given an order for rifles. The same firm received a timber-cutting contract worth from $300,000 to $500,000. Foote, with the backing of the State Department, refused to countenance a request for the propagation of any single Christian sect in Korea to the exclusion of others. So the summer and early fall passed in a familiar legation routine. The political situation in Korea seemed quiet. The pending war between France and China gave rise to the hope that it might force China to withdraw her troops from Korea. But aside from that there was little surface indication of the storm that was to break in a few months.

In the beginning of September, 1884, Foote prodded the State Department upon the matter of advisers. The delay of nearly a year in answering his No. 32 had both embarrassed and mystified him. He had not written oftener upon the subject because he had been cut off from communications from December 30, 1883, to March 1, 1884. Foote felt that the influence of the United States should become a permanent factor in the progress of Korea and was confident that the Department felt the same way. Young Koreans, educated in the Military School at Tokyo, were awaiting American instructors. Four thousand new American breech-loading rifles were stacked awaiting the arrival of American instructors. Other nations were seeking this privilege for the officers of their countries. The King impatiently awaited the arrival of Admiral Shufeldt who had promised to return in an advisory capacity.[28] However, Shufeldt had become coy, remaining silent on a proposal telegraphed by the King offering him all expenses and a salary commensurate with his position. "His Majesty has waited so patiently for nearly

---

[27] No. 70, Foote to Freylinghuysen, April 29, 1884.
[28] No. 105, Foote to Freylinghuysen, September 3, 1884.

Introduction

one year in his determination to have Americans fill these places, putting aside persistently pressure from all other sources."[29]

While Foote was thus writing there was, in transit, news which was to cause him to resign his position. The State Department appropriations for the fiscal year, 1884, had reduced the grade of his office from Envoy Extraordinary and Minister Plenipotentiary to that of Minister Resident and Consul General. No reduction in salary accompanied this change but both Foote and the Department were aware that a reduction in titular grade alone would make his position untenable, "owing to the widely different views attached to such things in the East."[30] For the Koreans would not understand why the United States should send them a Minister of the first rank and then degrade him.[31] This news on top of the inadequate arrangements for compensation made Foote decline the new appointment but offer to remain until a successor could be appointed.[32] The Department agreed to this and to relieve his feelings permitted him to return on leave of absence rather than resign in Seoul.

Meanwhile Foote had found out that Shufeldt would not come to Korea and, the patience of the King of Korea being exhausted, "years will hardly suffice to regain the advantages which we have thus voluntarily surrendered."[33] On November 5, 1884, Foote received his first direct answer on the matter of advisers. Freylinghuysen advised that the Department was aware of the urgency of the situation and had presented the matter to the Secretary of War *but this action had just been taken because for nearly a year Foote's dispatch No. 32 of October 19, 1883, had been mislaid*. Nor was Foote's cup yet full. The Congress adjourned without authorizing an appropriation for the purchase of a legation or the payment of Scudder. Foote, sans appropriation, put the Legation property in his own name. He could have disposed of it at a good price but refrained lest he discredit the United States.[34] For this transaction Foote has been attacked as a speculator who used diplomatic privilege for his own ends.

On December 4, 1884, gentlemanly recriminations between Foote and the Department were interrupted by the fact that on that evening revolution broke out in Seoul. At a dinner party attended by Foote, Aston, the Japanese Secretary of Legation, the Chinese Commissioner, Von Möllendorf, and the

---
[29] No. 110, Foote to Freylinghuysen, September 17, 1884.
[30] No. 10, Freylinghuysen to Foote, November 5, 1884.
[31] No. 112, Foote to Freylinghuysen, September 17, 1884.
[32] *Ibid.*
[33] No. 124, Foote to Freylinghuysen, November 15, 1884.
[34] No. 121, Foote to Freylinghuysen, October 15, 1884.

President and Vice-President of the Korean Foreign Office, an attack was made on the life of Min Yong Ik.[35] This was the first blow in an armed revolt led by "ill-advised young men dissatisfied with the non-progressive spirit of the past."[36] The first thought of the foreign representatives was to avert a clash between Chinese and Japanese troops in Seoul. On December 6, the mob, chanting "death to the Japanese," burned the Japanese Legation. The King, desperate over the intimation of renewed Chinese influence and the certainty of Japanese retaliation, asked Foote to go to Chemulpo to tell the Japanese Minister that Korea desired to maintain friendly relations with Japan. Foote did this and was next asked by the King to invoke the good offices of the United States in keeping the peace. The King also telegraphed directly to Washington to request the use of these same good offices.[37] The desperation of the King and the scene in Korea is well summed up by Foulk.[38] Between 1882 and 1884 the King had abetted the work of the progressives in Korea. In anticipation of getting American advisers he had dismissed Von Möllendorf from his post as Adviser to the Foreign Office and had also dismissed his Chinese military advisers. Arms had been purchased and stored away under Foulk's direction. But the delay in sending Shufeldt or other advisers had placed the Korean Government in an uncomfortable position. For, having cleared the Chinese out of the Army and the Foreign Office, it had no replacements. Unable to mark time under Chinese pressure the King had reappointed Von Möllendorf and the Chinese advisers in the fall of 1884. In October, 1884, the King told Foulk that without foreign intervention the Chinese would regain their lost ground and the small "progressive" coterie would be lost. On October 26, Foulk was told that an armed clash was inevitable. It came six weeks later in the form of a revolt.

On December 29, Foote returned from Chemulpo to Seoul to advise the Korean Foreign Office that prudence and conciliation were the means to conciliate Japanese anger.[39] The situation was delicate. There were rumors that Chinese troops were arriving at Masampo. It was a fact that 5,000 troops were accompanying Count Inoue, the Japanese Special Imperial Ambassador. Foote conferred with Inoue and advised him, "that any adjustment which involved the disintegration of Korean territory, would, in my opinion, be most unwise."[40] Inoue was willing to accept an apology and an indem-

[35] No. 127, Foote to Freylinghuysen, December 5, 1884.
[36] No. 128, Foote to Freylinghuysen, December 17, 1884.
[37] No. 20, Freylinghuysen to Foote, January 7, 1885.
[38] No. 128, Foote to Freylinghuysen, December 5, 1884, and enclosure by Foulk.
[39] No. 135, Foote to Freylinghuysen, December 29, 1884.
[40] No. 138, Foote to Freylinghuysen, January 2, 1885.

Introduction

nity. When it was found that the Chinese also desired an amicable settlement the tension eased in Seoul.[41] On January 9, 1885, Korea and Japan concluded a convention allowing Japan an indemnity for losses suffered during the uprising of December, 1884.

There were, however, more important results from the revolt. The Chinese had committed themselves to the statement that they had no power to settle any dispute arising between Japan and Korea. The King of Korea was forced to turn his government over to the conservative ministerial faction. The leaders of the revolt fled to Japan. A by-product of the actions of Foote during December, 1884, was an increase in the amicable relations between Japan and the United States. Foote had sheltered Japanese in the United States Legation during the bloody night of December 6 and had arranged for the safe escort of others to Chemulpo.

Foote's leave of absence was granted on February 4, 1885. George Foulk was left in the Legation as acting chargé. Confronted with the growth of reaction in Korea he took up the old problem of obtaining American advisers for Korea. The entire hope of the King seemed centered on this possibility. At the reception given the foreign representatives on the anniversary of the forty-ninth year of the dynasty, "the attention given to the representative of the United States was marked enough to be commented upon ... later."[42] The possibility of war between Japan and China was a Damocles sword over Korean autonomy. "Recognizing thoroughly its weaknesses and ignorance of the usages of war or of treating serious international questions, and admitting practically these and its fear of both Japan and China, the government proclaims in open terms, its wretched condition and seeks for aid from the representatives of the treaty powers now in Seoul."[43] "The most pressing need of Korea in her present deplorable situation is a number of competent Western instructors for her troops."[44] Of the two nations most interested in Korea one, Japan, approved of American instructors.[45] The continued request for advisers was met in one particular when three teachers were recommended to the State Department by the Bureau of Education of the Department of the Interior.[46] On May 15, 1885, Foulk wired the Department of State asking whether the Korean Government could wire advance passage money to prospective advisers. The King had invited Foulk to accept a sum sufficient to defray these expenses. "His

---
[41] No. 139, Foote to Freylinghuysen, January 4, 1885.
[42] No. 149, Foulk to Freylinghuysen, March 1, 1885.
[43] No. 152, Foulk to Freylinghuysen, March 9, 1885.
[44] No. 153, Foulk to Freylinghuysen, March 13, 1885.
[45] *Ibid.*
[46] No. 36, Bayard to Foulk, April 8, 1885.

Majesty informs me of his great embarrassment over the delay of a decisive response to his call upon the United States Government which was made in consequence of the offer of that Government expressed to the Korean Ambassadors to the United States repeatedly, to assist Korea to obtain competent assistants for its services. His Majesty always and frequently expresses in strong terms his preference for Americans to fill the positions referred to, but now states that his chief embarrassment is that he can make his calls for the assistants in any direction while that to America is pending. Having perfect faith in the United States Government, His Majesty believes that his call has been heeded."[47] To this the Department replied that Congress had not acted to authorize any Army officer to enter the service of a foreign country but that if the King desired the services of private citizens Foulk could so recommend, after getting permission from the Secretary of State.[48]

At this period Foulk seems to have been without funds or hopes of any. As acting chargé he could not draw his Navy pay. He was allotted half a minister's pay but was unable to draw upon any funds. This problem of finances was one reason for the eventual withdrawal of Foulk from his Legation duties because he could not meet the expenses of the Legation.

On April 28, Foote informed the Department that Von Möllendorf had been putting on pressure to get Germans into Korean service and that he had cast aspersions upon the United States, basing them upon the laxity of the United States in the matter of advisers and the manner of Foote's departure. The following month Foulk became aware of the most fantastic chapter of Von Möllendorf's career. "Prior to the Revolution of 1884 Von Möllendorf unquestionably had been the agent of China in Korea but had been held in check by the progressives. With the failure of the revolt and the withdrawal of the progressive leaders he began a most extraordinary and high handed career."[49]

The Korean Government, upset and angered by the English occupation of Port Hamilton, was ready to make a representation on the subject to the foreign representatives in Seoul. Foulk discovered that Aston had no idea of the feeling against England. Aston told Foulk that the occupation was temporary in "view of the outbreak of a great war with Russia."[50] Foulk then determined for himself, "that there must be some force at work among

---

[47] No. 171, Foulk to Bayard, May 15, 1885.
[48] No. 22, Bayard to Foulk with an enclosure from Bingham in Tokyo, May 18, 1885.
No. 24, Bingham to Foulk, June 4, 1885.
[49] No. 211, Foulk to Bayard, August 4, 1885.
[50] No. 172, Foulk to Bayard, May 19, 1885.

Introduction

them (the Koreans) tending to force Korea into partisanship in possible difficulties between England and Russia. Without doubt, as I have discovered, the attitude above referred to is due to Mr. P. G. Von Möllendorf, the Superintendent of Customs and the practical advisor of the Korean Foreign Office. This officer has stated to me that he has had negotiations with Russia several months ago, and knew with certainty that Russia would not make any occupation of Korean territory, implying certainly, that therefore, the entrance of English ships of war into Port Hamilton harbour must not be meant as a precaution against Russian occupation of that port, or any other near it, and must therefore be looked upon by Koreans as an act demanding explanation upon rigid call."[51] The Chinese had offered their aid to Korea on this matter which offer had the effect of irritating the Japanese. To Foulk the whole episode pointed out the inability of the Korean Government to rid itself of a pro-Chinese Foreign Office without the aid of Western advisers. This estimate was correct. The Chinese were preparing to return the ex-Regent to Korea. His enormous influence could be counted upon to build up Korean nationalism against Japan. Foulk was also correct concerning the intentions of Von Möllendorf. Russia had concluded a treaty with Korea in June, 1884, similar to those already concluded by Korea with England and Germany. But, unknown to the King and Korean Government, Von Möllendorf had conducted parallel secret negotiations by which Russia was to furnish instructors for the Korean Army and in return was to get the "loan" of Port Lazareff. To carry these terms into effect Alexis de Speyer, Secretary of the Russian Legation in Tokyo, arrived in Seoul in June, 1885, as "Agent Provisoir." He told Foulk that if England occupied Port Hamilton he was instructed to acquire "ten times as much territory for Russia."[52] Since the English were making permanent installations at Port Hamilton, it seemed as if de Speyer would carry through his instructions. This would mean the end of Korean independence. In this crisis the King of Korea begged Foulk for American advisers and, since the presence of Americans in Korea would seem to mitigate the growing Russian and English influence, "the Chinese and Japanese representatives here have called upon me to say that they have urgently advised Korea to secure the services of American assistants if possible."[53] It should be pointed out here that American military instructors did not arrive in Korea until April, 1888. For four years the Government of Korea, battered by internal dissension and torn between China and Japan on the one hand and England and

[51] *Ibid.*
[52] No. 180, Foulk to Bayard, June 16, 1885.
[53] No. 183, Foulk to Bayard, June 18, 1885.

Russia on the other, had been trying to save her shreds of autonomy by placing her affairs in the hands of neutral advisers. The net result of American delay was to shake the confidence of Korea in the United States and to make the United States impotent in East Asiatic affairs for another decade.

In July, 1885, Foulk found out from de Speyer that the Russian Government had now discovered that the secret negotiations of 1884 for furnishing Russian drill instructors to Korea was the work of Von Möllendorf alone. The Russian Minister to Tokyo, who had handled the negotiations, was unaware of Korean affairs, unaware of the Korean request for American advisers, and unaware that Von Möllendorf was acting on his own. "M. de Speyer states that he is now aware that the subject of employing Russian officers in Korea was originated and negotiated upon by Mr. Von Möllendorf wholly without authority, and wholly unknown to any Korean native official."[54] However, since the Emperor of Russia had already acted upon the treaty, "it is with strong feelings of deep embarrassment that he contemplated reporting to his government the turn affairs have taken; and he ventures to express the opinion that Russia may force Korea to accept Russian officers."[55] From de Speyer Foulk guessed that the whole tenor of the Russian negotiations was to establish Korea as a protectorate of Russia and, without speedy action by the United States, Korea would be forced to accept Russian advisers.[56] When the Korean Government became alert to the audacious conduct of Von Möllendorf it reported the whole affair to Li Hung Chang, the man responsible for placing Von Möllendorf with the Korean Government. On July 27, 1885, Von Möllendorf, with the acquiescence of China, was dropped from his Foreign Office post.

Not all of Foulk's activities in this period were concerned with such high affairs of state. He was still in a financial morass. He was involved in complicated negotiations involving indemnities for the old General Sherman case. He was hiring school teachers for the Korean Government. He was embroiled over a contract held by an American company to cut timber in Korea, which contract had been ignored by Von Möllendorf. Von Möllendorf became so objectionable over this that Foulk formally demanded his dismissal. All in all, he was busy conducting the constant routine of a legation while, at the same time, handling affairs generally reserved for an embassy. This was done almost single-handedly; for a study of his dispatches during these troublesome times seldom reveals him receiving

[54] No. 192, Foulk to Bayard, July 5, 1885.
[55] *Ibid.*
[56] *Ibid.*

Introduction 15

anything more pertinent from the Department than comment that his dispatches had "been perused with interest."

Meanwhile Korean internal affairs were at a boil again. In July, 1885, a Home Office was created which tended to centralize control of Korea in the palace.[57] Von Möllendorf had remained in Seoul as head of the customs service and maintained an active correspondence with Russia. Korea was making only feeble protests to England on the occupation of Port Hamilton regarding that occupation as a check against Russia. Then Von Möllendorf was dismissed from the customs which were placed directly under Sir Robert Hart of the Chinese Maritime Customs. Li Hung Chang, distrustful of Hart and determined to reassert complete Chinese hegemony over Korea, sent an American in Chinese service, O. N. Denny, as adviser to the Korean Foreign Office. This gave Li two powerful levers in Korea, Denny and Yuan Shih K'ai. Amid all this Japan remained a passive observer. With the installation of the conservative and pro-Chinese Min Yong Ik as commander in chief, China had control of Korean troops in Seoul. There were rumors that the ex-Regent would return and there was a good deal of nervousness over the rumor that the exile Revolutionary Kim Ok Kiun was using Japanese money and advice to prepare another revolution. The King on his part still hopefully awaited the arrival of American advisers. When both Chinese and German firms applied for mining permits he postponed action until some competent American could be there to advise him.[58]

The extent of Foulk's influence with the King may be seen in a dispatch of his which reported the substance of a dispatch from the English chargé to the Korean Foreign Office. "In explanation of my being aware of the substance of this dispatch, I may say that I have read the original of it: there had been made an error in the translation which accompanied it, and in the absence of any person in the Government who could clearly understand the meaning intended, I was asked to translate, and in this was shown the dispatch and translation."[59]

On October 3, 1885, the ex-Regent returned in style, guarded and accompanied by Chinese troops. It was a time of apprehension. "Among the officers of the Government anxiety amounting almost to consternation is evinced."[60] A new Russian chargé had arrived as well as a new Inspector General of the Customs, a new Chinese Commissioner and a new British

---

[57] No. 205, Foulk to Bayard, July 23, 1885. See also No. 214, Foulk to Bayard, August 16, 1885.
[58] No. 220, Foulk to Bayard, August 31, 1885.
[59] No. 223, Foulk to Bayard, September 1, 1885.
[60] No. 237, Foulk to Bayard, October 14, 1885.

representative. The new customs head was an American, H. F. Merrill, charged by Sir Robert Hart with seeking a union of the Chinese and Korean Customs. Hart, supposedly the neutral head of the Chinese Customs, was using his influence to play the Chinese-English game in Korea. The only note of relief in the picture was the new Russian chargé, I. Waeber who, in seeking the right of overland trade for Russia and a trading post on the northeast border, was mild and reasonable in his negotiations with Korea.[61] On October 15, 1885, Foulk reported what seemed to be a decisive step in the attempt of China to take full and undisputed control over Korea. Yuan Shih K'ai was sent to replace the Chinese Commissioner for Trade in Seoul.[62] Yuan had been chief of staff of the Chinese garrison at the time of the abortive revolt of 1884. As he assumed his new post he told Foulk that since Denny had been sent to Korea on the summons of China he, Yuan, would see to it that Korea would implicitly follow the advice of Denny. "This remark was extraordinary to me in that it was the first positive utterance of a Chinese official I have heard to the effect that China would not permit Korea to be free in her foreign and internal affairs. Nevertheless it has long been apparent to me that China controls Korea with an oppressive and strong hand."[63]

At this critical moment Foulk had the unpleasant experience of having his pay drafts returned owing to insufficient funds. The appropriation for Korea had been exhausted. "The Department fully appreciates your position in Korea and regrets that there was no other course open to it in the matter of your present draft."[64] To add to his difficulties he was under the necessity of handling matters at Chemulpo as well as at Seoul since the United States was the only country without a consul at Chemulpo.

Foulk had an audience with the ex-Regent who was closely watched by the Chinese although treated by them with great deference. His return had opened a new phase in Korean politics. Heretofore the great allies of China in Korea had been the house of the Queen. But, being deadly enemies of the Regent, they had broken with China over his return. Foulk's impression of the Regent was that the man was unable to keep out of politics and was therefore a potential source of trouble.

On the same day he made this report Foulk again requested clerical assistance, lack of which had placed him in "humble and humiliating circumstances."[65] On October 21, 1885, Foulk requested to be relieved of the charge

---

[61] No. 238, Foulk to Bayard, October 14, 1885.
[62] No. 240, Foulk to Bayard, October 15, 1885.
[63] *Ibid.*
[64] No. 74, Parker to Foulk, September 24, 1885.
[65] No. 244, Foulk to Bayard, October 20, 1885.

Introduction

of the Legation.⁶⁶ No particular cognizance was taken of this dispatch by Washington. A month later Foulk heard from Bayard merely that the Department was in receipt of his dispatches Nos. 236–249 which are the dispatches covering this period.⁶⁷ From now on until the spring of 1886 Foulk was to pursue a hopeless course in his efforts to uphold both the integrity of Korea and the integrity of the United States Foreign Service.

Yuan Shih K'ai had been given the title, "His Imperial Chinese Majesty's Resident in Korea." This title was the clue to the true relationship of China with Korea. In an interview with Yuan on November 23, 1885, Foulk established that China now considered herself in absolute control of Korea. "Mr. Yuan replied that China did not wish an advisor for Korea at present and none would be invited; that in compliance with a request of the King of Korea, he (General Yuan) had been appointed to this post in Korea and he would be the advisor to the King and government, assisted by the foreign representatives whom he would consult. Mr. Yuan went on to state that he had been specially instructed to maintain warm relations with the United States representative in Seoul and requested me, with seeming earnestness, to assist him by consultation, adding that he was not familiar with diplomatic usage. I then referred to the title written upon his card, asking him if he was to be regarded as 'Resident' in the sense of that word as applied to the English officials who reside with the Rajah and other native chiefs of state in the Residencies in India. To this question Mr. Yuan did not give a direct reply but instead a general one to the effect that the King of Korea would submit questions of state to him and he would consult with the other foreign representatives particularly myself."⁶⁸ Foulk also found that an envoy previously sent by the King of Korea to China, there to telegraph directly to Washington a request for speedy action on his numerous requests for advisers, had committed his message to Li Hung Chang. Li had acted to forestall American aid by immediately appointing Denny. The hapless King had accepted Denny having heard that he was an American of superior qualifications and character. Denny did not come at once for Yuan took over the post. With Yuan in as "Resident" the King again begged Foulk for American advisers! With Korea, for all practical purposes, a province of China and with his own position almost untenable, Foulk, as the representative of the United States, was still the lodestar of hope for the independent-minded group in Korea. "The above narrative well illustrates

---
⁶⁶ No. 246, Foulk to Bayard, October 21, 1885.
⁶⁷ No. 83, Bayard to Foulk, December 18, 1885.
⁶⁸ No. 255, Foulk to Bayard, November 25, 1885.

the embarrassing position in which I am constantly being placed in Korea, and I may trust, will show how great the necessity is for being explicitly instructed by my government. Because I am able to communicate with Koreans perhaps more readily than other foreign representatives here, and of my long residence in Korea, and the very favor in which I stand with a large body of officials, I am forced into a prominence hardly commensurate with such prudence and farsightedness as I may have acquired in my short experience in diplomatic duty."[69] What made Foulk all the more uncomfortable was the fact that he, in 1884, had been interpreter between the Korean Embassy and the Secretary of State and Assistant Secretary of State when the latter two had given advice and suggestions to the Embassy regarding advisers. "It is in consequence of my having occupied that position that my present one here is embarrassing and difficult in treating the numerous importunities of the Korean Government to be furnished assistants from the United States."[70] These advisers not forthcoming the King finally appointed the waiting Denny. The usefulness of Foulk was over. The Chinese, with tacit backing from England, had taken over Korea. So closely were the two operating in Korea that a mere rumor that Kim Ok Kiun was leaving Shimonoseki for Korea was sufficient to bring both Chinese and English gunboats to Chemulpo.[71] The Korean Customs under Merrill was regarded by English and Chinese authorities as a branch of the Chinese customs, "the head of which, Sir Robert Hart, is most actively engaged in political affairs of China and England. The most cordial relations here are being maintained between the head of the customs, Mr. Merrill, the Chinese Representative Yuan, and the British Consul General Mr. Baber; the general line of conduct and speech of these officials would prompt the inference that they are disposed entirely to ignore independent action of the Korean Government and to support the ruling of China in all matters of importance pertaining to Korea."[72]

On February 18, 1886, Foulk resigned. His reasons were a recapitulation of his and Foote's troubles. The inability of one man to carry the load without clerical or secretarial assistance, the insufficiency of the money appropriated to meet even the minimum expenses of a legation and, in Foulk's case, very ill health.

Three weeks after Foulk's resignation was accepted William Parker was confirmed as Minister to Korea. In acknowledging Foulk's resignation, "I

---
[69] *Ibid.*
[70] No. 257, Foulk to Bayard, December 1, 1885.
[71] No. 265, Foulk to Bayard, December 29, 1885.
[72] No. 272, Foulk to Bayard, January 18, 1886.

Introduction

can only repeat what then (no. 100) was said, that the Department sympathizes with you in the many embarrassments which you have been forced to encounter and fully appreciates the intelligent and zealous attention to the public interests which has characterized your official acts."[73] Foulk carried on until the arrival of Parker. There was a considerable amount of Legation minutiae to take care of; favorable reports on the activities of American missionaries and their hospital, various settlements and claims, renewed trouble with China—Denny, the adviser of Korea and agent of Li, had suddenly turned and become an advocate of Korean independence. This brought Yuan into the open. "China aims at something at least akin to incorporation of Korea into her own Empire...it comes too late and must fail."[74]

When Parker arrived the King asked Foulk to stay on in the Korean Civil Service. Foulk however left for Japan to rest. But his stay was cut short. Parker was inefficient and worse—he was generally helplessly drunk.[75] He was recalled and Foulk took over, for a second time, as acting chargé on September 3, 1886. Foulk left Korea for the last time a year later on the formal complaint of Li that he, along with Denny, was encouraging Korea on a course of independent action. The Korean Foreign Office backed Li although the King secretly implored Foulk to stay in Korea. Foulk was recalled although his conduct was approved by the Department of State.

The initial period of Korean-American relations had closed, however, with the first resignation of Foulk. The efforts of both Foote and Foulk to keep Korea independent had failed by the spring of 1886 when China achieved direction of Korean affairs. The United States had fumbled an opportunity that would not again be offered.

[73] No. 107, Bayard to Foulk, March 31, 1886.
[74] No. 297, Foulk to Bayard, April 23, 1886.
[75] No. 2, Foulk to Bayard, September 7, 1886.

1.

THE UNITED STATES LEGATION IN SEOUL

NO. I.   Department of State
                                                    Washington, March 9, 1883
Lucius H. Foote Esqr.

Sir:

Congress having authorized the maintenance of diplomatic relations with the Governments of Eastern Asia, and the President by and with the advice and consent of the Senate, having appointed you to be the Envoy Extraordinary and Minister Plenipotentiary of the United States to Corea, I have now to enclose to you the following documents.
1. Your commission in that capacity.
2. A letter of credence addressed to His Majesty The King of Chosen, with an office copy of the same, which you will communicate to the Minister of Foreign Affairs, upon your asking through him an audience of His Majesty for the purpose of presenting the original.
3. Copy of the printed Personal Instructions prescribed by this Department, for the government of our diplomatic officers abroad and copies of two recent circulars amendatory thereof, dated respectively, May 12, 1881, and April 9, 1882.
4. Copy of Consular Regulations of 1881.
5. Special passport for yourself and suite.
6. Register of the Department of State.
7. Blank form of oath of Office which you will properly execute and return to this Department.

Your salary will be at the rate of $5000.00 per annum.

You will be allowed compensation at the same rate for such time as you shall be actually and necessarily occupied in receiving your instructions, not exceeding thirty (30) days, to be settled at the Department before your departure, and in making the transit between your place of residence and your post of duty at the commencement and termination of the period of your official service, not in excess of seventy days going and returning.

You will therefore be careful to inform the Department of these dates.

You will also be allowed the sum of $3,000.00 yearly for rent, and contingent expenses of your Legation and for the services of a clerk and Interpreter.

For your salary as it falls due quarterly and for the contingent expenses and rent of your Legation you will draw upon the Department of State, you are also authorized to draw upon the Secretary of State for the amount to which you will be entitled for the time occupied in receiving your instructions previous to your departure for your post of duty.

You are referred to Section XXXII to XL inclusive, of the printed personal instructions and to the circulars mentioned for detailed information and direction as to the mode of drawing your salary and of rendering your accounts as well as for the regulations relating to the expenditures of your Legation.

The present being the first mission established by this Government with that of Chosen, there is, of course, no precedent, to guide you concerning your diplomatic correspondence, and your own judgement and discretion must therefore be relied upon in the premises. Your former Consular experience will no doubt materially assist you in the discharge of these new and important duties. Special instructions upon important subjects between the two governments, will be sent to you, from time to time as occasion may require.

The Department entertains the confidence that your intelligence and zealous attention to the interest of the United States now confided to your care will be eminently conducive to the harmony and friendly relations existing between the two countries which it is so much the desire of the President to maintain and strengthen.

Fredk. T. Frelinghuysen

NO. 3.   Department of State.
Washington, March 17, 1883.

Lucius H. Foote, Esq.

Sir,

You have already received the general and formal instructions given to a Minister of the United States about to proceed to his post and it now remains for me to supplement them by more specific information made necessary by the peculiar nature of your mission.

You are the first Minister from the United States and so far as is known from any western Power accredited to Corea. You will of course impress the Government with the conviction that it is with no ulterior design that the United States seek to cultivate friendly relations with it.

Your attention will be directed to the relations between Corea, China and Japan—a subject not without difficulty.

United States Legation in Seoul

The treaty between the United States and Corea provides that the "High Contracting Powers may each appoint diplomatic representatives to reside at the court of the other" and each may appoint also consular representatives. The preamble of the Treaty states that "the United States of America and the Kingdom of Chosen being sincerely desirous of establishing permanent relations of amity and friendship between their respective peoples, have to this end appointed * * * the King of Chosen, Shen Chen, President of the Royal Cabinet, Chin Hong Chi, member of the Royal Cabinet, as his Commissioners Plenipotentiary." It will be seen from these extracts as well as from the tenor of the treaty that the negotiations were conducted as between two independent and sovereign nations, and it is further to be remarked that the Chinese officials were familiar with its terms and in a friendly manner aided the representative of this government.

The Treaty was, however, accompanied by a letter from the King of Chosen to the President in which occurs this statement: "The Chou Hsein country (Corea) is a dependency of China, but the management of her governmental affairs, home and foreign, has always been vested in the sovereign." It appears also that the King of Corea assents that the Treaty be acknowledged and carried into effect according to the laws of independent states and that in questions between Corea and China this Government "shall in no wise interfere." The relations of the United States towards Corea are therefore clear. As far as we are concerned Corea is an independent sovereign power, with all the attendant rights,—privileges, duties and responsibilities: in her relations to China we have no desire to interfere unless action should be taken prejudicial to the rights of the United States.

In this connection it becomes important to examine certain so called trade regulations between China and Corea, recently promulgated, which may give rise to discussion. A copy of them is herewith enclosed and your attention is particularly directed thereto.

You will note that the preamble contains the statement that the canons of official intercourse between Corea and China are fixed, and they are accepted as a fact. Bearing in mind that the negotiation of the regulations was carried on in careful conformity to these canons much light is thrown on the relations between the two countries.

The preamble contains no declaration that the King of Corea acted either in his sovereign right or of his own option in the appointment of envoys to negotiate the regulations, which it is also to be remarked contain no stipulation providing for their ratification or rejection by the King, while on the contrary Article VIII provides that the Regulations shall go into effect at once and amendments may be discussed between the Superintendant of Northern Trade of China and the King of Corea acting as equals (for this is the force of the Chinese text) their conclusions to be submitted to the Emperor of China.

There is nothing to show that in the negotiation of these regulations the King of Corea had any independent control beyond the nomination of the negotiators who were practically controlled by the Chinese Superintendant of Northern Trade.

The regulations further provide that the Superintendant of Northern Trade shall correspond on terms of equality with the King of Corea, and while the King of Corea shall send an envoy and commercial agents to China the Chinese agents are to be accredited to Corea not by the Emperor but by the Superintendant of Northern Trade, a subordinate official. The Corean envoy also is to reside at Tientsien, not at the capital, his rank is assimilated to that of a consul and he can address only the Superintendant of Trade and then—as an inferior.

While certain distinctions of rank in China do not assimilate to analogous distinction in Western countries the broad fact remains that in these regulations the King of Corea is treated not as a sovereign but as the equal only of a high but subordinate official of China.

As to the relations between China and Corea we have, as I have already remarked, no immediate interest, but should the Chinese or Corean officials attempt by analogy to diminish the respect with which you are to be treated, and because the sovereign to whom you are accredited is treated as a subordinate, attempt to treat you as an agent sent to a subordinate, a different state of affairs will immediately be presented. You will then remember that for all purposes of intercourse between the United States and Corea the King is a sovereign, and that with sovereign states only do the United States treat. Further the representatives of the United States in China will treat the Corean representatives there as in the position assigned them by the Chinese government, first because of the statement of the King of Corea in his letter to the President and secondly because a state having the inherent right to decline to receive diplomatic or consular representatives in the absence of treaty, has no less the right within proper limits to affix the condition of their recognition. The Chinese commercial agents in Corea will be treated by you as subordinate officials appointed by a subordinate officer and not bearing the commission of the Emperor. As these agents are understood to have only commercial duties it is not supposed that you will be obliged to hold any official communication with them, and therefore no difficulty on

United States Legation in Seoul

that score is to be anticipated. Should any arise you will apply to this Department without—delay for further instructions.

The last clause of the preamble to the regulations declares that they are to be regarded as so many concessions on the part of China "and are not within the scope of the Favored Nation rule existing between the several Treaty Powers and China." The right of Coreans to trade in Peking seems to be the only concession in the regulations not already found in treaties with the Western powers, and this clause so restricts the concession that it is not apparently of much force. Remark upon it however is reserved until reports from you shall have been received by which we may obtain a clearer understanding of the situation.

This question of trade and of the rights of the United States in relation thereto should receive your careful attention. By the Treaty between the United States and Corea our citizens may establish themselves at such Corean ports as are open to foreign trade. These ports are not specified in the Treaty but are understood to be those opened to the Japanese—viz. Fusan, Ren-Chuan and Yung Ling, and also Yang-hua, to be opened within one year by virtue of the Convention of August 30, 1882 between Japan and Corea. Chinese subjects are allowed to establish themselves and to follow their vocations at all these ports and also to reside in the two suburbs of Seoul and at two trading posts in the interior. Americans may not travel in the interior, while this privilege is allowed to Chinese. By virtue of a stipulation in the Japanese Convention operating through our Treaty with Corea, diplomatic and consular representatives of the United States may travel in the interior under passport. Chinese may transport merchandize to the four points in the interior and may at any place in the interior purchase and bring out native produce paying only an export duty. These privileges have not been granted to Americans.

Citizens of the United States are also forbidden to transport native produce from one open port to another open port, a privilege accorded to Chinese under certain restrictions. As to this your attention is called to the resolution of the Senate which accompanies the treaty. The import duty taxed on Chinese importations is less than that taxed on American importations, and it is impossible to learn from the regulations whether the duties and tonnage dues taxed upon Chinese discriminate against the trade of the United States.

Briefly the following privileges are denied to citizens of the United States and allowed to Chinese:

1. To reside and trade at four points in the interior.
2. To travel in the interior under passport.

3. To take foreign produce to four points in the interior and to proceed to the interior and bring out native produce.
4. To transport native produce from one open port to another.
5. A discrimination of 1/2 in one case and 5/6 in the other to our disadvantage and to the benefit of Chinese importers in the duties on all foreign merchandise imported *via* certain routes into Corea.

These concessions to China are extremely important. With the enormous advantage thus given them it is apparent that Chinese merchants will have a practical monopoly of Corean trade. To this the United States cannot consent and while the relations of China and Corea may not be of importance to us and while in the treatment of Coreans in China, or the rank of Chinese officials in Corea we are not interested, this practical abolishment of the rights secured to us by Treaty can not be assented to. For the present it may not be advisable to take any active steps in the matter as the participation of western nations in Corean trade is looked upon with jealousy by a large party, but your attention will be given to the matter as soon after your arrival as possible. Your reports on this subject will be anxiously awaited that further instructions may be given to you based upon fuller and more accurate information. As at present informed it seems that the broad provisions of Article XIV of the Treaty secure to us the privileges granted to China in the Commercial Regulations.

As you are aware the ratifications of the Corean treaty (of which a copy is enclosed) are to be exchanged at Yin-Chuen on or—before the 22nd of May next it will therefore be your duty to reach that point at as early a date as possible that all proper preparations may be made for the exchange which you will make on behalf of the United States. Your powers therefor are enclosed.

It is expected that you will leave San Francisco by the steamship of the 29th instant, you will be met at Yokohama by a vessel of the Navy of the United States which will convey you to your port. The Treaty will be found at the Legation in Japan where to avoid possible accident or delay it was carried by the Secretary of Legation who recently proceeded to his post. It is advisable for you to see Mr. Bingham while in Japan and to converse freely with him as to your mission: it is not doubted that his good judgement and trained experience in Eastern affairs will be of advantage to you. You may also read to him confidentially these instructions and the copy of the President's letter to the King, and should he desire it allow him to retain a copy of each for confidential use and you will deliver the enclosed instruction No. 722 addressed to him.

Before exchanging the ratification of the Treaty you will call the attention of the appropriate authorities to the resolution of the Senate in relation to vessels proceeding from one open port to another. The propriety of this stipulation is too apparent to make any argument in its favour necessary.

As to your personal movements and method of communication with this Government it is impossible to instruct you. Speaking generally it is hoped that you may be able to remain as constantly at your post as do other Ministers of the United States, at the same time the peculiar difficulties attending the residence of a foreigner in Corea are appreciated and due allowance made therefor.

It is said that a Chinese line of steamers will soon connect the capital with ports in China; should this be true you will be thus furnished with convenient means of communication with this Department and your colleagues in the East. Meantime it may be necessary for you to ask the aid of the officers of the United States Asiatic Squadron which it is not doubted will be courteously afforded you as far as is within their power.

Briefly then your mission is

1st To exchange the ratifications of the Treaty after securing the King's consent to the interpretations of the Senate.

2d To cultivate friendly relations with the Government and people of Corea, to allay jealousy and convince them of the amicable sentiments of the United States.

3d To report fully as to the relations of Corea, China and Japan that appropriate steps may be taken to secure for our citizens the privileges granted to the Chinese in the Commercial Regulations.

4th. To inform this Department fully as to all matters of political importance or of interest to those engaged in commerce; and you will from time to time send here for publication any information which may promote trade between the United States and Corea.

A letter from the President to the King of Chosen in answer to those which accompanied the Treaty, together with an office copy thereof, are herewith enclosed. The former you will deliver in the usual manner.

It is suggested that you confer from time to time frankly and freely with your colleagues in China and Japan on all matters touching the relations of Corea to these countries.

Fredk. T. Frelinghuysen

NO. II. Confidential June 30. 1883

Secretary of State

Sir,

In an interview today, with the Chief of the Foreign Office, the matter of Trade Regulations was informally discussed. I took the occasion to say that it was understood by my Government, that certain exclusive rights and privileges had been granted to a neighboring power and that while the United States did not desire to make undue exactions, that she must insist that all privileges granted to other nations, should be conceded to her. In view of the facts, it is difficult to understand by what right China demands these commercial advantages. It is even difficult to conceive how she can consistantly insist upon her claim of suzerainty,(After having induced Corea to make treaties with the Western Powers.) Evidently the Corean Government feels and fears the omnipresent espionage of China.

Lucius H. Foote

NO. 15. Department of State,
Washington, August 17, 1883.

Lucius H. Foote, Esqr.,

Sir,

I have to acknowledge the receipt of your No. 10, of June 29th last, wherein you report having taken up your permanent residence at Seôul. Whatever regrets the Department may feel at the personal discomforts of your present situation, as you report them, it can not but commend your decision in selecting Seôul as your place of residence, as the wisest under every possible circumstance.

Alvey A. Adee
Acting Secretary

United States Legation in Seoul

NO. 17.   *Confidential*   July 19, 1883

Secretary of State

Sir,

I find that the King manifests great interest in all the details of his government. On several occasions of late, I have received Messengers direct from His Majesty asking information and even advice upon minor matters. These questions have pertained particularly to the methods of raising revenue in the United States. My advice has also been sought in reference to the granting of Special privileges for mining in Corea. I fully appreciate the delicacy of such a position and have on each occasion replied guardedly and in general terms. It seems to me that such contingencies are neither to be sought for, nor avoided, and whenever they occur, I shall deem it a duty to report them to you.

Lucius H. Foote

NO. 21.   Department of State,
Washington, Sept. 18, 1883.

Lucius H. Foote, Esqre.

Sir,

Your No. 17 of July 19th, touching the disposition of the King to solicit your advice in matters affecting the internal development of Corea has been received.

In fully approving the discretion manifested by you in meeting invitations of this nature the Department remarks that, while there is no objection to your giving to the King personal suggestions in such matters, they are to be regarded as personal only when not expressly covered by instructions from here.

Fredk. T. Frelinghuysen

NO. 17. Department of State,
Washington, August 17, 1883.

Lucius H. Foote, Esqr.,

Sir,

Your despatches numbered 9, 10, 11, 12 and 13, have been received.

Your No. 12, of the 1st ultimo, refers to Chinese officials in Corea, which was the subject of Mr. Young's No. 135, a copy of which was sent to you, and I desire to say that the Department approves the discretion you evince in treating matters affecting the relations of China and Japan with Corea, to which, at this distance of time and place, much must be trusted.

Alvey A. Adee
Acting Secretary.

NO. 27. Department of State.
Washington, Oct. 16, 1883.

Lucius H. Foote, Esq.,

Sir:

As the visit of the Special Mission which His Majesty the King of Tah Chosun has been pleased to send to this country, is now drawing to a close the Department deems it proper to communicate to you officially some of the incidents connected with their reception at various places in the United States in order that you may be informed as to the cordial welcome which the members of the Chosunese Special Mission have received in the principal cities of this country, and as to the gratification which their friendly visit has afforded to this government and the American people.

Upon the arrival of the Special Mission at San Francisco on the 2nd day of September, 1883, they received from Major General John M. Schofield, of the Army of the United States, the highest marks of respect, and on the 4th of the same month the San Francisco Chamber of Commerce and the Board of Trade, jointly, gave them a reception, on which occasion they were formally welcomed to the city and met the prominent merchants and business men of San Francisco.

From San Francisco the Special Mission came east by the Central and Union Pacific Railroads and arrived at Chicago on the 12th of September, where they were officially received by Lieutenant General P. H. Sheridan, of

United States Legation in Seoul 33

the United States Army, who did all in their power to make their brief stay in that city agreeable by causing them to be properly accompanied to various points of interest there.

When the Special Mission left Chicago for Washington on the evening of the 13th ultimo, Lieutenant General Sheridan, as a mark of respect, detailed Colonel Gregory of his staff, to accompany them to the National Capital.

The special Mission arrived in the city of Washington, on the 15th day of September, 1883, and were at once quartered at the Arlington Hotel as the guests of the Government. On the same day they were presented to Mr. Davis, Acting Secretary of State.

Upon the arrival of the Special Mission at the capital, the President directed Lieutenant Mason and Ensign Foulke, of the United States Navy, to assist in rendering suitable attentions to them as the guests of this government.

These officers and Mr. Davis, Assistant Secretary, accompanied the Special Mission to New York where they were met by the Secretary of State who presented them to the President, at the time temporarily in that city. The presentation took place on the 18th ultimo. The press report of the proceedings on that occasion is herewith enclosed, in which you will find the address made by the President at the time.

On the same day, September 18th, the Special Mission still escorted by the officers detailed to accompany them, took passage for Boston by the Fall River Line, arriving in that city at 7 A.M., on the following morning. During the day they inspected the Foreign Exhibition and the Manufacturers' Institute.

On the 20th of September, the model farm of M. J. W. Wolcott, was visited to witness the use of the latest agricultural emprovements and to inspect the farm buildings. On the same day the Special Mission were taken by railway to Lowell where the members were shown the process of manufacturing cotton goods in the Roalt Mills, of carpet making in the Merrimach Manufacturing Company's Mills, of making print goods in the Lowell Manufacturing Company's Mills, and of the manufacture of knitted underwear and hose in the Lawrence Manufacturing Company's Mills. The Manager of Ayre's Patent Medicine Works, also opened their establishment to the inspection of the Special Mission.

On September 22nd calls were made upon the Governor of Massachusetts and the Mayor of Boston and various public institutions of the city were inspected. During the afternoon the members of the Special Mission were entertained at the home of Mr. Lowell, the Foreign Secretary of the Mission, and on the 24th of September they returned to New York.

In advance of the arrival of the Special Mission at New York, Commodore John H. Upshur, of the United States Navy, Commandant of the Brooklyn Navy Yard, after conference with the city authorities and the merchants of New York, prepared a programme of excursions and visits for the entertainment and instruction of the Special Mission, in pursuance of which they visited and inspected among other places and institutions the New York Hospital, the Western Union Telegraph Office, the New York Fire Department, the Post Office Building, the establishments of Tiffany & Co., the Cramp Docks, Havermyer's Sugar Refinery, the offices of "The Evening Post" and "The New York Herald," the Brooklyn Navy Yard and the Military School at West Point.

On Saturday, September 29th, the Special Mission took their departure from New York and arrived at Washington in the afternoon where they still remain. Since the Special Mission returned to this capital, every facility has been afforded them to become acquainted with the practical workings of this government.

Previous to the final departure of the Special Mission from this city, they were accorded a farewell audience with the President, at noon, on the 12th instant, when the Secretary of State again presented them to the President and the several members of his cabinet who were in attendence at the Executive Mansion. The Minister Plenipotentiary gratefully made his acknowledgement to the President for his kindness and the many acts of courtesy, both official and private, which he and the other members of the Special Mission had enjoyed during their sojourn in the United States. At the conclusion of this interview the Secretary of State at the request of the President, tendered to the Minister Plenipotentiary and any two others of the Special Mission, whom he might name, passage on board of the U.S.S. "Trenton" which is soon to depart for Corean waters. This offer was accepted and the necessary orders were at once given to the Secretary of the Navy for their return to their native country in accordance with this desire of the President.

The other members of the Special Mission will leave Washington to-day en route for San Francisco, from which point they will embark on board of a steamship for the East.

Fredk. T. Frelinghuysen

United States Legation in Seoul

NO. 28. Department of State,
Washington, Oct 23, 1883.

Lucius H. Foote, Esq.,

Sir:

With his No. 247, of the 1st ultimo, Mr. Young, the United States Minister at Peking, has transmitted to the Department, copies of certain correspondence received by him from our Consulate at Chefoo, relative to the Roman Catholic Faith in Corea. Mr. Young observes that he had furnished you with copies of those letters. For that reason I do not now inclose copies of the same, and think it only necessary to remark that the general propaganda of foreign faiths is not deemed a proper subject for inclusion in any treaty, but that freedom to follow the dictates of their own consciences must be secured to all American citizens in Corea. Believing as this Government does, that the toleration of faiths is the true policy of all enlightened powers, this Department would be glad to see you extend your good offices within proper grounds and counsel the Coreans to treat all missionaries kindly.

Fredk. T. Frelinghuysen

NO. 34 Seoul
Oct. 23, 1883

Secretary of State

Sir:

Upon my arrival in Corea I found a Mr. Von Mollendorff acting in the capacity of adviser to the Foreign Office. For certain reasons, not necessary to explain, he has seemed to feel that there should be no intercourse with the Government excepting through his intervention. On several occasions he has endeavored to restrict me by reference to the "Shufeldt Treaty," and has of late advised the Government that, under our treaty I had no right to interpose objections, or to make suggestions in regard to the General Trade Regulations which the Government of Corea proposes to decree. One of the principal points which I have sought to secure, is that the American Trade Dollar shall be received in payment for duties, fees, etc.

In an interview yesterday with the Minister of Foreign Affairs, the Under Secretaries, including Mr. Von Mollendorff being present, I was endeavoring to explain my views, when reference was again made to the "Shufeldt

Treaty"; I said with some degree of firmness, "Mr. Minister, I desire to say a few words. The Treaty between the United States and Corea, was ratified by my Government when Great Britain and Germany declined to ratify a similar treaty. It was accepted with no thought of Commercial gain. My country cares very little for your commerce, Sir. The treaty was ratified because the United States thought it might be of some service to Corea, in entering upon her new relations with the World. It seems, however, of late, if the Representative of the United States open his mouth upon international questions, the "Shufeldt Treaty" is thrust down his throat. Now, Sir, if that treaty is to prevent friendly intercourse between your government and mine, we had better tear it up and throw it into the Sea." The result was, as I anticipated, that everything asked for was conceded, without a dissenting word. To comprehend the necessity of such talk, the circumstances and the character of the people must be considered.

Within ten days I hope to transmit to you a Copy of the Corean Trade Regulations and Rates of Tariff.

Lucius H. Foote

NO. 58.　　　　　　　　　　　　　　　　　　Department of State,
　　　　　　　　　　　　　　　　　　　　　Washington, July 14, 1884.

Lucius H. Foote, Esqr.

Sir:–

The diplomatic and consular appropriations act for the current fiscal year, approved July 7, 1884, reduces the grade of your office from that of Envoy Extraordinary and Minister Plenipotentiary to that of Minister Resident and Consul General, without change of salary.

A new commission and instructions will accordingly be sent to you at the earliest date possible.

You may say, however, to the Government to which you are accredited, that no disparagement of Corean dignity or want of appreciation on the part of the United States is implied by the change, but simply that Congress has sought to make the diplomatic service more uniform as to rank and salary.

Fredk. T. Frelinghuysen

United States Legation in Seoul

NO. 112. September 17, 1884.

Secretary of State

Sir:

I have delayed replying to your No. 58. for a day or two, that I might carefully consider the subject and act only after mature deliberation; and now, having decided, I may perhaps be permitted to say some things which otherwise would not be relevant; and first, I desire through you, Sir, to express to His Excellency the President my sincere thanks for this renewed manifestation of his confidence, in tendering to me the appointment of Minister Resident and Consul General to Corea: and to you Mr. Secretary I can only say that I fully comprehend and appreciate the firm faith which you have manifested in my integrity, and perhaps in my capacity, and I am aware Sir, that this is not due to political influence, but rather the result of higher considerations, for which, in a marked degree the present administration has been distinguished. The position I have held has not been devoid of difficulty and has required the exercise of a certain degree of tact and discretion, in order to secure that confidence which would insure success.

If I have in any manner succeeded, it has been with the sole purpose of extending the influence of my country and of opening new fields for her commerce. I should have been glad to have remained long enough at my post to have seen certain things accomplished and to have aided perhaps in their accomplishment; and I must feel that Congress has to some extent shorn me of my strength. Of course you will quite understand that, in my own estimation, the change in the rank detracts nothing from the character of the position; its importance is to be measured only by the amount of Service which the Minister is capable of rendering to his country: but to these people, proud that the United States should have sent to them a Minister of the first rank, it is impossible to explain the reasons for the change, without leaving the most unfortunate impressions, while the Minister degraded in their estimation by the loss of his rank, is no longer clothed with the same importance and influence. Another and minor consideration, and one which I mention only for the benefit of those who succeed me, is the inadaquacy of the compensation. Living is necessarily expensive in the East, and more so in Corea than in China or Japan, because the supplies are brought from those countries at an increased expense. For these reasons I must respectfully decline the appointment which His Excellency the President has so graciously tendered to me.

My present status is seemingly somewhat anomalous, but believing that there must be some provision for such cases, or some precedent to govern them, I shall continue the functions of the position until further advised.

Lucius H. Foote

NO. 10.
Department of State,
Washington, Nov. 5, 1884.

Lucius H. Foote, Esqr.

Sir:

I have to acknowledge the receipt of your No. 112, of September 17th last, declining the appointment as Minister Resident and Consul General to Corea, and giving the reasons which control your action.

I can confidently assure you that the Department greatly regrets the loss of your services and appreciates the ability and energy with which you have invariably discharged your official duties.

I beg to suggest that in order to avoid embarrassment on your part which the reduction in your official rank might possibly occasion and of which you felt assured, owing to the widely different views entertained of such things in the East, and to avoid, also, the not improbable misunderstanding on the part of the Government of Corea were you under the circumstances, to endeavor to explain the action of Congress respecting such change, you avail yourself of a leave of absence with permission to come to the United States, when the further course of this Government in the premises can be discussed.

Fredk. T. Frelinghuysen

244 Oct. 20, 1885

Secretary of State

Sir:

I would respectfully ask the attention of the Department to the fact that as yet there has been no provision made, that I am aware of, for a secretary or any clerical assistant to the United States representative to this country, and would urgently beg to suggest that the necessary steps be taken to provide for such at the earliest opportunity.

While the interests of the United States in Korea may be regarded as small, and the actual secretary's work or that of a clerical assistant correspondingly insignificant, it yet remains a fact that out of considerations of the early stage of development of Korea, embodying a life of isolation in a measure, and extraordinary difficulties in maintaining a respectable livelihood that provision of an assistant to the representative here may be regarded as an absolute necessity to him.

As regards my own experience, I may say that having some knowledge of the language of Korea and of its customs, I have been able to live here, yet in a humiliatingly humble way, and with much vexatious difficulty. Certainly to any other incumbent of the office who will necessarily be wholly unprepared in language, and in other respects as well, the difficulty of living here and maintaining an establishment... [MS breaks off here]

George C. Foulk

NO. 85.   Department of State
                Washington, D. C.
Ensign George C. Foulk, U.S.N.   January 18, 1886

Sir:

I have to acknowledge the receipt of your despatch No. 251 of November 17, 1885, reporting your successful intervention with the Government of Korea to secure the grant of a franchise to fish for pearl oysters on the Korean Coast in favor of W. A. Newell, an American citizen. As a general rule it is undesirable that a legation abroad should appear to advocate concessions or exclusive privileges of trade or business in favor of its countrymen. This government is always well pleased when the legitimate enterprise of the U. S. Citizens is recognised, or rewarded by foreign governments, but it cannot be expected to show an interest in the success of any particular project. All this government asks is fair and equal treatment of its citizens.

The department views herein given are advisory merely as to future occasions of this nature. There is no purpose to condemn your reported action which seems to have been characterized by your usual good discretion.

James D. Porter
Acting Secretary

NO. 279   February 18, 1886

Secretary of State

Sir:

It is with regret that I have to say that the circumstances under which I have served the Department of State in charge of this legation during the past year has been such as to render me in a great measure unfit for such further duty, and I must request that the Department provide a relief to take charge of the legation.

The state of affairs in Korea has been one of excitement and gravity, such as to necessitate unceasing observation and watchfulness, and an amount of office work and embarrassing duty, in other respects, which I have only been able to execute under constant and severe strain. It is simply impossible for one person to execute for any length of time, without clerical assistance, the work called for at this legation.

The pay of Chargé d'Affairs ad interim is wholly insufficient to meet the necessary expenses of such an officer living here in charge of the legation, yet I have been unable to secure even this for a period of six months, through the return of my drafts Nos. 18 x and 19 x. In addition to these facts, it may be considered that Mr. Foote left the legation without providing means for me to live here in charge, and the legation household establishment unprovided with many of the barest necessaries for living in it; and also, that I assumed charge of the legation immediately after my personal effects and outfit for living in Korea had been stolen and destroyed by the Korean mob in December, 1884.

Though I have become embarrassingly in debt personally, I have been forced to deny myself reasonable and necessary comforts of living, and in addition have suffered constant humiliation, personally and in consideration of my official position through the spectacle unavoidably presented in this connection by myself to the native and foreign communities here.

For the past five months I have been in ill health, and recently have only resisted my inclination to leave Korea upon a medical certificate by the hope that each steamer might bring me a relief.

My commission in the Navy precludes my being regularly installed here as Chargé d'Affairs ad interim, yet the years service I have rendered as in charge here, and the character of work now being called upon to perform by the Department of State place me in effect and appearance as the regularly installed Chargé. My taking up the duty under the exceptional circumstances attending Mr. Foote's departure from Korea, was to me an imperative duty, accepted without question or doubt, under my obligations as an officer of the Navy, but I would respectfully submit protest against being thus kept retained in the position beyond the time necessary to have a regular appointment to this mission made.

George C. Foulk

NO. I. September 2, 1886

Secretary of State

Sir:

I beg to inform you that I arrived in Söul on yesterday, the 1st. instant at 6 PM and at once relieved Mr. Wm. H. Parker, Minister Resident and Consul General, of the charge of this Legation, as directed by the Department in its instructions sent me through our legation in Tokio.

Telegraphic communication with China hence had been cut off for some ten days past, and Minister Parker received his telegraphic recall only a few hours before my arrival at the legation; he had however been informed that his recall was enroute by the Commanding Officer of the U.S.S. Ossipee several days before.

Minister Parker will leave the legation tomorrow morning to take passage aboard the "Ossipee" for Yokahama. Under the circumstances attending his recall he waives audience with His Majesty and further communication with the Foreign Office of Korea.

I have this date addressed a communication to the President of the Foreign Office informing him of my instructions from the Department and Minister Parker's recall and asking for an interview with him at the Foreign Office: in this communication I subscribed myself as chargé d'affaires ad interim.

Affairs in Söul are very quiet. The effect of the recent political disturbances created by the Chinese representative has doubtless been to increase the difficulties attending the status and future of Korea. On this subject I shall later address a fuller report.

George C. Foulk

NO. 2.   Legation of the United States
                         Söul, Korea
Secretary of State   September 7, 1886

Sir:

In addition to the content of my dispatch No. 1, Dip. Series, dated Sept. 2d instant, I have the honor to report the following to respect to my relieving Mr. W. H. Parker of the charge of this Legation.

On August 21st last, while I was at Takeo, in the interior of Japan near Nagasaki, I received word that important telegrams awaited me at Nagasaki. A Typhoon having come on on that date, my arrival in Nagasaki was delayed until the night of the 23rd of August. I found the following telegrams awaiting me at our consulate at Nagasaki:

From: Minister Hubbard, Tokio—dated 20/8, 7/50.
"I am directed by the department to say that you are to take charge of the legation at Söul Parker recalled davis will send ship to Chemulpo have asked him to take you over communicated with davis at once by wire. Hubbard."
From: Admiral Davis, Shanghai dated 20/8, 9/25 P.
"Do you need Ossipee now Chefoo for conveyance Korea if not she can meet you Chemulpo. Davis"

On Aug. 24th, I telegraphed to Admiral Davis at Shanghai: "Passage Ossipee from Nagasaki no other steamer till first. foulk", in reply to which Admiral Davis telegraphed me, "Ossipee Chemulpo wires down can you come here Marion will take you Chemulpo davis."

I then telegraphed Admiral Davis on Aug. 24th, "Go Japanese steamer first September quickest. foulk." On Aug. 25th Admiral Davis telegraphed me—"I go Nagasaki for you Thursday. davis."

On Saturday Aug. 28, the "Marion" with Admiral Davis on board arrived at the mouth of Nagasaki harbor, at about 8 P.M. I went on board at once with my effects, and the "Marion" sailed at 10 P.M. for Korea.

Arriving off Chemulpho at 3 P.M. Aug. 31, I landed at once; as I left the ship the honors accorded to a Charge d'Affaires ad interim by Naval Regulations, including a salute of eleven guns, were executed by direction of Admiral Davis.

Telegraphic communication with Korea having been interrupted for a considerable period, the particulars of a reported political disturbance in Korea had not reached the Admiral at Shanghai, nor myself at Nagasaki. On shore, at Chemulpo, upon inquiry at the English and Japanese Con-

United States Legation in Seoul

sulates, I learned certain details of the affair, and that cholera had practically disappeared from the Capitol district. I telegraphed to Minister Parker—

"Arrived in Marion with Admiral. I come Söul tomorrow alone for charge."

On the following day I left for Söul, my conveyance having been very courteously arranged for by Suzuki Mitsuyoshi, the Japanese Consul at Chemulpho. On the way to Söul I was met by an officer dispatched by His Majesty the King to welcome me. Other officers came with messages from his Majesty after I had reached the legation.

While at Nagasaki I had received letters from Koreans and Americans in which reference was made to the deplorable condition of this legation while in Mr. Parker's hands.

I find these reports more than corroberated. The Minister has been intoxicated during a considerable part of his residence here. Korean and Foreign officials ceased to visit him. Judge Denny informed me the King had proposed asking our government for the recall of Mr. Parker. During the recent political disturbance foreigners were filled with apprehension; the Americans came to the American legation for advice and found the minister drunk. Nearly all the correspondence relating to the summoning of the Ossipee from Chefoo, and the guard of Marines from that ship to the legation was performed by the American residents, the Minister merely affixing his signature. There would seem to have been no necessity for the coming of a guard of Marines from Chemulpho, and the action is disapproved of by nearly all the officials, Korean and foreign, I have met, as having only tended to create suspicion and excitement amoung the people who were quiet. I learned that the Korean Foreign office objected to the presence of an armed force, quoting the provisions of the convention at Tientsin between Japan and China, by which neither China nor Japan could send troops to Korea without notifying the other; in reply to this the Foreign Office was informed from the legation the 20 Marines from the "Ossipee" were merely a guard or escort to the Commanding Officer of that Vessel Comdr. Mc Glensey. This reply I deem to have been a grave error: it tends to suggest a precedent to be used against receiving armed protection in Söul for the legation and armed citizens here. The marines having come to Söul, they might have been returned speedily, but leaving the salutary impression on Koreans and Chinese that our government was vigilant in the protection of its citizens here. Such an impression may, in a degree, have been left, but in a weaker form than it might have been.

I endeavored to effect Mr. Parker's departure from Söul as quickly as possible. He left the city on the morning of Sept. the 3d. I telegraphed his departure to Comdr. McGlensey of the "Ossipee" and he was received on board that vessel immediately on his arrival at Chemulpho.

I am informed that the "Ossipee" sailed on the 4th instant direct for Yokohoma.

In my dispatch number 1, I stated Mr. Parker waived further correspondence with the Foreign Office. After writing the dispatch, I prevailed upon him to send a dispatch I had prepared to the Foreign Office, announcing his recall and my assumption of charge of the legation.

I beg especially to ask the Department's attention to the very great and courteous assistance rendered me by Admiral Davis. The attentions he has shown me must have benefited me very greatly. His promptness in the duty he undertook has had a doubly good result, in that he arrived off Chemulpho at an early moment after the recent political disturbances in Söul, and irrespective of the benefit I may have received, his presence there with the "Marion" and "Ossipee" formed a demonstration productive of good effects in our relations with Korea, assisting me to recover the position so much injured by the conduct of the legation in Mr. Parker's hands.

George C. Foulk

NO. 58.
Ensign George C. Foulk, U.S.N.

Department of State,
Washington, July 31, 1885.

Sir:-

I herewith enclose a report of the Law Officer of this Department, dated July 24, 1885, and the memorandum upon which it was based, in the case of the "General Sherman", concerning which you made a report to the Secretary of the Navy, on the 29th of March last.

At the time of the destruction of the vessel and the death or subsequent execution of those on board, Corea was under the qualified suzerainty of China and the claim for indemnification for these offences of the Coreans was submitted to that government. China, however, disclaimed responsibility for the offences of the Coreans, alleging that her suzerainty over Corea was simply ceremonial. This disclaimer was accepted by the United States, and as this Government had not established diplomatic relations with Corea,

United States Legation in Seoul

the matter was permitted to rest. But nothing has occurred, so far as appears from the correspondence on the subject, to release the Government of Corea from liability for whatever losses and injuries may have been sustained by our citizens in the destruction of the "General Sherman" and the death or putting to death of her crew.

You are, therefore, instructed to inquire into the circumstances of the case, and if the ascertained facts bear out the statements heretofore made, to ask from the Corean Government such indemnity as may seem proper. The lapse of time which has occurred since the commission of the alleged offences against the "General Sherman" and her crew, cannot affect the validity of whatever claim there may originally have been against the Government of Corea, especially as this Government is now availing itself of the first opportunity it has had to seek a peaceful settlement.

A full report of your action is awaited.

T. F. Bayard

REPORT NO. 118.   Law Bureau, July 24th. 1885.

To the Honorable

The Secretary of State.

Subject, Claim against Corea on account of the destruction of the "General Sherman" See mem. dated July 23, 1885.

Sir:

The present claim is based upon an alleged massacre of the vessel "General Sherman" at Corea in 1866. The facts of the case as far as they are understood, are given in the annexed memorandum prepared by Mr. Cridler, of the diplomatic bureau. The failure heretofore to obtain diplomatic action on these facts has arisen from the circumstances that until a comparatively recent date we have had no diplomatic representative in Corea. Since, however, Mr. Foulk is now at Corea as Chargé d'Affaires, it is now recommended that this report with the accompanying papers be sent to him with instructions to inquire into the circumstances of the case and to ask for such indemnity as may be proper.

All of which is respectfully submitted.

Francis Wharton.
Solicitor, e c.

It appears that Messrs. Meadows and Co., a British firm of Tientsin, were the charterers of the vessel and that they leased her with a cargo of merchandise for sale in Corea. Their letter of Dec. 27, 1866, with Mr. Burlingame's No. 126, gives the particulars of their enterprise and its disastrous result. Their letter was as follows:

"As the act of visiting Corea for the purpose of trade was not an act which could, in the eyes of civilized Western nations justify the Corean Government in destroying those who committed it, we, the undersigned, have taken the liberty of addressing you for the purpose of bringing the above matters to your Excellency's notice, with the request that you be pleased to beg his Excellency Admiral Bell to make inquiries regarding the destruction of the vessel and her people and take steps to cause the Corean Government to make redress as far as such in the nature of things is practicable."

The Consul of the United States at Cheefoo, writing to Mr. Burlingame, under date of October 30, 1866, says:

"The "General Sherman" left here on the 9th. August; she called for water; took Mr. George Hogarth (British subject) as supercargo and Rev. Mr. Thomas (British) as interpreter. The owner, W. B. Preston (American) also went with them—Page,—Captain, Wilson, chief mate (both American). The crew consisted of 18 or 20, Malays and Chinese. Cargo, cotton goods, glass, tin plates, &c. &c.

Mr. Burlingame brought the matter to the attention of the Government of China, on the ground that Corea was formerly tributary to China, but Prince Kung, promptly disavowed all responsibility for the act of the Coreans or jurisdiction over them, stating that the only connection between the two countries was one of ceremonial. Afterwards Mr. Burlingame acquainted the commanding officer of the United States Asiatic squadron, with the reply of Prince Kung and asked that a vessel of war be sent to Corea to ascertain the facts of the case "to the end that they may be reported to the Government for its instructions". The mission of Admiral Bell failed of its result, however. Again in 1868, Mr. Williams sought the good offices of the Chinese Government in ascertaining by direct application to the King of Corea what were the real circumstances connected with the loss of the *Sherman*. The reply of the Corean Government, however, disclosed nothing tangible.

With this it would seem, that our efforts ceased in respect of direct application to learn anything regarding the destruction of the vessel or the murder of her crew. But it may be incidently remarked that afterwards several

United States Legation in Seoul

visits by different persons acting under instructions from this Government were made to Corea to obtain information in regard to the country, but they met with but indifferent success and their reports throw no new light on the *Sherman* disaster. An attempt was also made in 1870 to secure a treaty with Corea for the protection of shipwrecked mariners on her coast, but this proved unsuccessful.

As regards the independence of Corea, so far as her Governmental policy is concerned, it may be observed, that the United States Government recognized this position, when in 1882, May 23d., Admiral Shufeldt negotiated with the Kingdom a treaty of Peace, amity, commerce and navigation, although the good offices of China were sought and obtained to contribute to the success of the negotiations so far as were deemed practicable.

Miss Preston's letter refers to the published narrative of Ensign Foulk, and adds "I consider that the Coreans treated my father not only cruelly but also unjustly and think the Government should be compelled to pay the loss. x x x x x Please send me word if I can forward any claim on the loss of his life or vessel."

In this view of the case, the question becomes one for Dr. Wharton's consideration. He should say whether it is now in order to press a claim on Corea as Miss Preston asks. I have endeavored only to give Dr. Wharton an idea of the history of the case and the previous diplomatic steps taken to effect its settlement.

The lapse of time, as well as the mystery surrounding the circumstances of the affair, except so far as the loss of a vessel and the murder of her crew appear evident, may make it difficult at this late date, to properly represent the matter diplomatically to Corea. However, the moral obligation of Corea is as great to-day as at any previous time; and having a Legation at Seoul, at present, any prosecution of the matter which may be decided upon, will not encounter the embarrassing circumstances which were unavoidably associated with the former prosecution.

(Original account furnished by Ensign Jno. B. Bernadon U. S. Navy)
Narrative of the Destruction of the Schooner Sherman

The Sherman arrived at Peng Yang in August, 1866, and anchored in the Taitong river below the city on the Peng Yang side. Midsummer is the time of the chang ma or heavy rains which come annually at this season along the Yellow Sea coast of Corea. The rain falls almost incessantly for ten or fifteen days, the lowlands are flooded, the rivers rise many feet and navigation for the clumsy Corean boats becomes practically impossible.

The Sherman was seen from the city walls and was the cause of much excitement; but on account of the dangerous condition of the river, which was then very high, no boat ventured in her. Finally, when the water began to subside, Pak-tjong-houn, the Kamsa, or provincial governor, sent officers to enquire her mission. The common people took advantage of their departure to gratify their own curiosity, and a large fleet of small boats put out from the shore.

The Sherman's people, not understanding what was being done considered this as a hostile demonstration, and on their approach fired several shots into the air. at once the officers turned back accompanied by all the others.

But the river fell rapidly and in a few days the Sherman went aground. Efforts to get her afloat were unsuccessful and she careened over; this was seen from the walls and the city was once more in excitement. Another fleet of boats came towards her, this time with hostile intent, the people being armed; shots were again fired and they turned back as before.

Both officers and people were now enraged and an attempt was made to destroy the vessel; and which was successful. Boats were loaded with cumbustible material, which were taken to points above her anchorage, their contents were ignited and they were allowed to drift down; and soon the Sherman was in flames. The crew jumped overboard to save themselves, but most of them were drowned; a few were picked up however by the Corean boats, which put out immediately after them. Among these was an European, known to the Coreans as Tchoi-nan-en, who was able to communicate with the officials.

The prisoners were brought before the Kamsa and examined. They told the object of their coming and tried to explain why a white flag had been waved on the vessel upon the approach of the fireboats; and they asked that they should be taken to China and surrendered there. All efforts on their part were useless, however, and in a few days they were led out from prison and beheaded.

The above is a narrative of a Corean Christian, told me at the time of my trip to Peng Yang. Tchoi-nan-en, was probably the Rev. Mr. Thomas, who in expressing his name in Chinese characters may have used the first syllable of his surname to correspond with the Chinese *seung*.

Note on "Sherman" affair—

The account obtained by Ensign John B. Bernadon, U. S. Navy,—sent to Navy Department by Ensign George C. Foulk.

The Sherman arrived off Peng Yang in Aug. 1866—was visible from the walls which were thronged with people, upon and after her arrival—to look at her. It was the time of the *Changma*, or heavy summer rains, and the river was very high. Officers took boats to go onboard to inquire of her mission, crowds of people went along out of curiosity to see the stranger. The Shermans people apparently became alarmed at the great crowd approaching and a musket was

United States Legation in Seoul

fired, (in the air). At this the officers & people (Koreans)—turned back. After this the Korean officers & people again started for the Sherman, & turned back as before when the musket was again fired. The river then began to fall (or was already falling) and the Sherman went aground and careened over on her side. The people, greatly incensed & excited sent fire-rafts down stream upon the *Sherman*. She caught fire & burned up—was destroyed. Her people jumped overboard—some drowning, while others were picked up & taken to the Kamyon (Governor's house). They were given a hearing, & asked to be sent to China. One of them know Chinese and was named Choi Nan Un. Their entreaties were not heeded & in a few days they were led out and executed.

B G.C.F. in a conversation with Chön Yung Muk a *Chusa* (title-official)—of the Royal Hospital, referred to the Sherman affair. Chön Yung Muk, several days later stated to G.C.F. that he had spoken to the King of the Sherman affair & my remarks on it to him and he (muk) stated that His Majesty deplored the affair greatly—that he (King) was then very young and did not have any active part in affairs, which were conducted by the Tai Wön Kun. The King also mentioned a *gun* (cannon) of the Sherman which is yet at Peng Yang, and that one of the Shermans people named Choe Nan Un (which Muk says may be written [Chinese character]) was a mightily strong man and fought bravely, giving much trouble to his captor's on the shore. The Governor at Peng Yang was = Pak = an old man, well educated, who knew something about foreign countries; he died long since.

C. From accounts of Chön Yang Muk & others I gather the following opinion of the state of the times &c. It was at about the time of the arrival of the *Sherman* that the Tai Wun Kun was exercising his tyrannical power at its full height—especially directing it towards Christians. A large number of Christians had been executed, including the Jesuit Priests of France. Thousands of people—not Christians, had been executed as suspects, and the system of ferretting out was still actively going on about Peng Yang numbers of people had been executed & the district was especially excited & terrified. All Korea recognized all foreigners as alike—as being of the hated Roman Church, and it was believed that except when driven by stress of weather, wreck &c., foreigners only came to Korea to aid the Roman Catholic cause. Nationally there existed a feeling that the deaths of the French Priests—& the general attack on Christianity might be the occasion for the coming of other foreigners to avenge their fellow Christians. Consequently when the *Sherman* appeared, there was but one thought among the Koreans—which was that she came to spread Christianity or to avenge the work against Christians which had been going on. There were all sorts of ill-defined fears excited by her appearance: some people, not at heart filled with hatred of the foreigners, were forced to think of destroying her & her people because their neutrality would make them appear as abettors of the foreigners designs and they might lose their head. In the terror & excitement which existed, there can be but little doubt but that *en masse* the people aimed at the destruction of the *Sherman* & even the best disposed at heart, dared not even express the thought of sparing her upon any explanation of her mission to be gotten by inquiry of the Sherman's people.

George C. Foulk,
Decr–Jany
1885 1886

D.   All Koreans questioned by me, state that the vessel was not plundered—but simply destroyed—cargo & hull. All the information I have obtained in Korea tends to this view.

George C. Foulk
Jany 23/86

E.   Undoubtedly to my mind, there has been from ancient times a strictly enforced law in regard to vessels in distress coming to Korean coasts. They were to be supplied with food & the necessary assistance, at the expense of the Korean Government, to depart safely. Officers were & are yet placed along the coast whose duty it is to inquire the business of strangers coming to their districts & to execute the laws in regard to vessels in distress. Chinese vessels on the West coast and particularly Japanese vessels on the East coast have in thousands of cases been assisted to return to their countries. *Samchok*, a port on the Japan Sea has been noted for centuries, as one to which foreign vessels (Japanese) have numerously been driven by stress of weather, &c.

George C. Foulk
Jany 26/886.

2.

SECURING AMERICAN ADVISERS FOR THE KOREAN GOVERNMENT

NO. 32. *Confidential* October 19, 1883

Secretary of State

Sir,

I was called on the 16th inst. to an audience with the King, and taken to apartments and grounds, to which, I was told, no foreigners had ever been admitted. After being ushered into the presence of the King, I was asked to be seated near to him, which I am led to believe is an unprecedented occurrance. Every person then withdrew from the Audience Chamber with the exception of the King, Myself, and the Corean Interpreter.

First enquiring after the health of His Excellency, the President of the United States, His Majesty said, "I desire, through you, to thank your Government, for the kind reception which my Envoys have received upon their arrival at San Francisco. I fully understand the disinterested policy of the United States; and I wish always, to rely especially, upon the advice and assistance of Your Government. The English and the Germans are about to send Commissioners here to negotiate new treaties, and I wish you, Mr. Minister, to give me such advice in these Matters, as may seem to you best. I believe that these treaties will tend to strengthen my Government, and I ask, that, if it can consistantly do so, the Government of the United States will urge Russia and France to enter into treaty negotiations with me."

His Majesty also said, "A Chinese Official is soon to arrive here. I wish to understand his relative rank, and if questions shall arise, I may ask your advice." He said further, "I desire the services of an American Gentleman, one who can write the Mandarin language of China, to act in an advisory capacity in my Office of Foreign Affairs; if your Government, or you, will designate such a person, I will give him the Second rank in that Office."

He also said, "I wish to procure the services of an American Military Officer, to instruct and drill my troops. If such an one can be recommended to me, I will confer upon him the Second Military rank in my Kingdom."

To the remarks of His Majesty, I endeavored to reply in an appropriate way. I assured him of the friendship which my Government felt for himself and his people, thanked him for the confidence which he had manifested in the U. S. and told him that I would at once refer these matters to you.

I said further, that, personally I felt highly gratified at this evidence of his esteem, and that whenever I could consistently, as the Representative of my Government, give to him any advice, I would freely do so.

This interview was more marked from the fact of its entire freedom from formality at a Court where formality is such a feature. When the exclusive character of this Sovereign is considered; his difficulty of access, even by his own people, it seems remarkable. His manner was exceedingly kind and cordial, and I was forcibly struck by the Knowledge of affairs which he manifested.

The influence of Foreigners holding confidential positions in these Oriental countries, seems to add largely to the influence of their respective Governments. In this view of the case, I may be permitted to urge, that, if consistent, persons may be designated for these posts, in compliance with the King's desires.

I should also be pleased to inform His Majesty, that my Government had called the attention of Russia and France to his sentiments in reference to treaty negotiations.

Lucius H. Foote

NO. 105.   Sept. 3, 1884

Secretary of State

Sir:

The long delay, nearly one year, in taking action upon matter referred to in my No. 32 has both embarrassed and mystified me. It seemed to me particularly desirable that the influence of the United States should be felt in the regeneration of Corea, and that that influence should become a permanent factor in her progress, and when at the instance of the King I wrote my despatch No. 32, I was confident that its importance would strike you and that my suggestions would be considered. To understand the reason why I did not sooner again call your attention to the matter, it must be borne in mind that from the 30th of December 1883 until the 1st day of March 1884, I was virtually shut in from the outside world and received no mails. Upon the return of Mr. Hong from his mission to the United States, he informed me that Admiral Shufeldt had expressed a willingness to visit Corea in an advisory capacity, if the Corean Government so desired. I could only reply that that matter had been submitted to my Government for consideration and that I could give no advice: in the meantime the King frequently manifested to me his anxiety upon the subject. Subsequently upon the arrival of the Trenton the matter was fully discussed and upon the request of His Majesty I telegraphed Admiral Shufeldt to come. The arrival of a Military Officer from the United States to organize and instruct the Corean Troops is anxiously hoped for. Fourteen young Coreans educated in the Military School at Tokio are waiting to assist him and four thousand stand at Arms,—Breechloading Rifles,—purchased in the United States, remain, by order of His Majesty, undistributed until he shall arrive. Men of other Nationalities, through the Officials of their respective Governments, are seeking these positions, and I would earnestly ask you to take immediate action in the matter.

I may mention, incidentally, that Mr. Von Mollendorff late Foreign advisor to the Corean Government has resigned and retired from the Foreign Office.

Lucius H. Foote

NO. 109. September 10, 1884.
Secretary of State

Sir:

The King has of late manifested much interest in the establishment of English Schools and has requested me to procure from the United States three teachers, Young Men preferred, to each of whom a monthly salary of $125, and an allowance of six hundred dollars passage money will be paid. He also requests me to obtain for him a Superintendant of farm work, one capable of taking charge of the Government farm which he is establishing. He desires a practical man. One who understands the breeding and care of cattle and sheep, the making of butter and cheese, the grafting of fruit trees & ec. To such a man a salary of $150. per month and $600. passage money will be paid. Of course these persons should be given to understand that the life they are coming to is not one of ease, and that they must be willing to submit to many inconveniences. I am induced to present such requests to you, from the fact that Mr. Foulke informs me, that, all aid was promised to the Corean Envoys in such matters by the Department of State.

Lucius H. Foote

NO. 110.   September 17, 1884.

Secretary of State

Sir:

Since writing my No. 105, a letter has been received from Admiral Shufeldt leaving the question of his coming to Corea somewhat in doubt; he urges the question of expense &c. The anxiety of the King is so great in the matter that Admiral Shufeldt has again been telegraphed to. His Majesty is equally anxious about the Military Officer and has waited so patiently for nearly one year in his determination to have Americans fill these places, putting aside persistently all pressure from other sources; that I sincerely hope there will be no delay in sending forward some Military Officer who can organize the Corean Troops, and if Admiral Shufeldt does not come, that some capable man may be designated to act as Advisor to the Corean Government. All expenses in coming will be paid and a fair salary commensurate with the importance of the position will be paid. I have already said so much upon this subject that it seems hardly necessary to add more. These places are to be filled by Americans or the subjects of some European Power, and I am assured that China and Japan will be satisfied if these positions are filled by Citizens of the United States.

                                                  Lucius H. Foote

NO. 124   Nov. 15, 1884.

Secretary of State

Sir:

Mr. Peanag Sic of late an Attache of the Corean Embassy to the United States, has just returned from Japan, and reports to the King upon information received from our Consul General at Yokohama, that Admiral Shufeldt will not come to Corea in an advisory capacity. Yesterday the King invited me to an audience, and informed me that the non compliance on the part of the United States, with his requests, as made known to you in my No. 32, dated Oct. 19, 1883, (more than one year since), had embarrassed him. The truth is that the King's patience is exhausted with the long delay and in the mean time those persons are not wanting who have intimated to him that, had he asked Great Britain or Germany, to perform a like service, it would have been done at once. The result will be that we shall lose that voice and influence in the Corean Government which it has been my constant endeavor to secure.

Years will hardly suffice to regain the advantages which we thus voluntarily surrender.

Lucius H. Foote

NO. 14 Department of State,
Washington, Nov. 6, 1884.
Lucius H. Foote, Esqr.,

Sir:

I have received your Nos. 105 and 117, of the 3rd and 17th of September last; also the copy of your No. 32 of October 19, 1883, the original of which has been mislaid. These despatches have reference to the employment of American Military officers in Corea to organize and drill Corean troops and to advise the government in respect of such things.

I have today fully and urgently presented the matter to the Secretary of War, in a letter summarizing your several despatches, and have asked that he give the subject his immediate attention and favor me with his response. Upon receipt of this, I will at once advise you of its purport.

The Department thoroughly appreciates all that you have said as regards the presence of American officers in Corea, as a means of strengthening our influence there, and regrets the accident by which the matter has been thus necessarily delayed.

Fredk. T. Frelinghuysen

NO. 171. May 15, 1885.
Secretary of State

Sir:

I have the honor to inform you that on April 26th ultimo, I despatched from Seoul, by letter to the United States Consul at Nagasaki, Japan, the following telegram, "Secretary State
   Washington
   May Korea wire passage Adviser military men urgent
        Foulk"

I had been repeatedly urged to receive a sum of money from His Majesty for transmission to the United States to defray the travelling expenses of the persons expected to come here for service under the Korean Government, as asked for by His Majesty in despatches No. 32—Oct. 19, 1883, and No. 109, Sept. 10, 1884, from this Legation—but declined to receive it, and do so yet.

The results of the conference at Peking between Japan and China render it imperative for Korea to secure the services of the persons asked for in No. 32, referred to above, and at an early date, as upon the removal of the Chinese and Japanese forces here, the country bid fair to be without either Chinese and (or) Japanese directive influence. His Majesty informs me of his great embarrassment over the delay of a decisive response to his call upon the United States Government which was made in consequence of the offer of that Government expressed to the Korean Embassadors to the United States repeatedly, to assist Korea to obtain competent assistants for its service. His Majesty always, and frequently expresses in strong terms his preference for Americans to fill the positions referred to, but now states that his chief embarrassment is that he can make his call for the assistants in any direction while that to America is pending. Having perfect faith in the United States Government, His Majesty believes that his call has been heeded, and recalling the urgent need of the assistants at the earliest practicable moment (date)—I have been asked to communicate by telegraph, as above reported, as a timely precaution to effect their speedy coming.

The whole Government evinces much anxious interest in this matter, and the foreign representatives have expressed their satisfaction with the prospect of the coming of these Americans.

George C. Foulk

NO. 184. June 18, 1885.

Secretary of State

Sir:

On June 8th instant, I received a communication from the United States representative in Tokio, Japan, which contained the following telegraphic despatch.

"Washington, D. C., 16th May, 1885–8ʰ–30ᵐ P.M.
Bingham, Tokio
Tell Foulk Congress took no action touching Army instructors.
                                                                Bayard."

Inquiries had been daily addressed by the Korean government as to the coming of an advisor and military instructors from the United States. Upon the receipt of the Department's reply to my telegram, I at once informed the President of the Office for foreign affairs of Korea of it, and on the 14th instant was summoned to a private audience with His Majesty, the King, at which he questioned me long and anxiously upon this subject.

While His Majesty manifested much disappointment upon learning the assistants could not be at once summoned to Korea, it was plainly intimated that he would continue steadfast in his resolve to have these secured from the United States while any chance remained of its possibility.

In speaking of this subject, His Majesty remarked upon the friendly offers of assistance made by the United States; upon its having made the opening treaty of the Western Powers with Korea, and spoke at length of the great benefit Korea must derive from the assistance of competent Americans only, at this time of her weakness amidst the threatening dissensions of the European powers. His Majesty closed his remarks by saying he would direct the Foreign Office to address a letter to the United States directly, with the hope of receiving an early and favorable reply.

I may add in connection with this, subject, that I have in my conversations upon it at the Foreign Office and as well, in the presence of the King, endeavored to dispel any idea the Korean government may entertain that it is bound to await the action of the United States government and thus while it may desire to apply elsewhere for assistants, feel not at liberty to do so.

The evidently much increased anxiety of His Majesty to have the American assistants is without doubt due to the attitude of Russia and England in their present strained relations; these are threatening to the autonomy of Korea; Port Hamilton is in the hands of England, and the Russian Agent here uses almost dictatorial language to Korean officials in expressing the intention of his government to secure Korean territory if England retains Port Hamilton.

The Chinese and Japanese representatives here have called upon me to say they have urgently advised Korea to secure the services of American assistants, if possible. The former has told me such advice has been by letter, conveyed to His Majesty from Li Hung Chang.
                                                                George C. Foulk

NO. 204   July 22, 1885.

Secretary of State

Sir,

Referring to the Department's despatch No. 36, dated April 8, 1885, in regard to school teachers for Korea, and the enclosures therewith transmitted, I have the honor to communicate the following in reply to the request of the Commissioner of Education for additional information as to the conditions of the service of the three teachers selected by him.

To obtain the desired information I addressed the President of the Foreign Office in writing and called upon him personally: his reply I received yesterday, a translation of it being as follows.

"Having referred your recent letter to our sovereign, His Majesty spoke com-"mendably of your words and directed me to reply.

"In regard to calling school teachers, now having discussed the subject, I beg "you to be informed as follows;

"1. In regard to the teaching, it will be done in school buildings to be furnished "by us (not in private families).

"2. A house to be used as the residence of the school teachers will be furnished "by us.

"3. Passage money (as for the teachers) will be allowed for the wife of one of "the teachers.

"4. The teachers to serve two years.

"5. The studies &c., to be determined when the teachers shall have arrived and "a discussion with them shall have been held.

"Irrespective of the foregoing, (we say), that the advisor asked for to your "Honorable government is now even more urgently desired than the teachers.

"An answer by direction of our Sovereign.

   "1885, 10th of July.
                   "Respectfully, Kim Yun Sik
                              "President of the Foreign Office.
"To Foulk, Acting Minister for the United States."

In addition to the above I may say that the buildings for the schools and residence of the teachers will be Korean ones; they may easily be rendered comfortable and serviceable.

There will probably be boarding pupils at the schools. To assist the teachers, a number of students who have been learning English at a school already in Seoul, will be detailed.

It has been intimated that should the American teachers be competent, they may be employed in other ways by the Government—as in assisting in starting a newspaper for Seoul, &c., than exclusively as school teachers.

There is already in Seoul a small colony of foreign residents, including several ladies. At Chemulpho most of the usual household necessaries may be obtained, and the stores there are improving. Steamers arrive at least twice each month. While the Koreans are very ignorant, their hospitality and generosity are great, and there is no question but that there is a wide spread desire to learn and improve among them.

The President of the Foreign Office has stated that he regrets that the Adviser asked from the United States could not have been secured before the teachers, and explains that it was the intention of His Majesty to have the Adviser and military instructors come first; with these the Government would have discussed and decided upon the necessary steps for improvement of the country, in the execution of which, the teachers, the farmer, and other assistants would be necessary.

George C. Foulk

NO. 257   *Confidential*   Dec. 1, 1885

Secretary of State

Sir:

I have the honor to acknowledge the receipt of the Department's confidential letter of instructions—No. 63, dated Aug. 19, 1885, relating to the intrigues of which Seoul has been the center and their bearing upon requests made to the United States Government by Korea to furnish military instructors.

I am pleased to state that I have heretofore acted in accordance with the instructions of the Department's late letter. I have long been taking pains to have it distinctly understood that our government in no sense originated or is disposed to press the proposal to obtain United States Military officers for service in Korea and am sure that this understanding is held by all the foreign representatives in Seoul and the Korean Government itself.

In this connection I would state however, that the requests for assistants of the several kinds to the United States Government addressed by His Majesty, the King of Korea, are undoubtedly largely based upon advice given and suggestions made by the Secretary of State and the Assistant Secretary of State to the Korean Embassadors upon the occasions of several visits to the Department of State when they were in the United States. Upon these occasions I acted as interpreter and it is in consequence of my having occupied that position, that my present one here is embarrassing and difficult in treating the numerous importunities of the Korean Government to be furnished assistants from the United States.

I have long since realized the great advantages to be derived from a correspondence upon Korean subjects with our representatives in Peking and Tokio, and am grateful for the instructions given by the Department to facilitate my establishing such.

George C. Foulk

NO. 9 October 3, 1886

Secretary of State

Sir:

I beg to inform you that under date of yesterday the President of the Foreign Office of Korea has addressed me a communication in which after referring to the application made two years ago to the United States Government to furnish Army officers to serve as Military Instructors *in Korea,* and the reply of the United States Government that Congress would be asked to pass the bill necessary to admit of the coming of the Army Officers, the President asked me to ascertain as to whether the officers are to come to Korea or not.

Almost daily inquiries as to the coming of these Army Officers have been addressed me by officers sent to the legation by His Majesty the King. In view of the activity of Russia at present, and the negotiations attempted by Mr. de Speyer to effect placing a body of Russian military officers in Korea, in July of last year, when those negotiations were chiefly defeated by the plea of Korea that the United States had long since been asked to furnish military instructors, the anxiety evinced here by the King and government of Korea is very great. It is known to His Majesty that the Congress has adjourned some time since and word as to what action has been taken by it in the matter of these instructions has been thus far vainly and with deep suspense waited for. No further delay in placing military instructors with Korean troops can be admitted. In case it is known definitely that the American officers are not to come, the government and

His Majesty evince desire to ask for German officers, but feel that this is checked in a degree by Russia.

There can be but little doubt but that the treaty power which furnishes military instructors to this country, will through them largely control advantages of every kind to be derived through relations with Korea by treaty. From the time it is definitely established in Korea that the United States cannot supply the officers applied for, we may expect our influence to wane here, and a very probable increase of the already grave difficulties besetting the little Kingdom we were chiefly instrumental in bringing to the notice of the world of nations.

George C. Foulk

NO. 10.   6 October, 1886

Secretary of State

Sir:

I have the honor to report that on the 3d instant I was invited to Audience—at the Palace—with His Majesty the King and the Crown Prince. At the Audience, His Majesty, after a most kindly reception stated that he had asked me to Audience to express his gratification at my return to Korea. I was asked many questions as to the position I held at the legation and the action taken by the United States Government upon his request that I be permitted to serve Korea. To these I could only reply that sufficient time had not yet elapsed to admit of my hearing by letter from my government, but that I would probably receive definite instruction by mail in a short time.

After the Audience His Majesty sent me word that in case the United States Government could not furnish the military officers asked by him, he requested me to use my own judgment and act personally to secure from America competent instructors for the Korean troops—representing that unless American instructors came to Korea, his government would have difficulty involving China and Japan over a possible attempt of Russia to place military instructors in Korea. On the 3d instant, I received a despatch from the President of the Foreign Office making inquiries after the military instructors. Again on the 4th instant, an officer was sent by the King to confer with me on this subject. I then decided to telegraph to the Department, and at 5:45 P.M. on the 4th instant, despatched the following telegram in cipher;—

Bayard, Washington
    Stigma betoken 20744 salivates taber namesake otherwise.
Seoul

    (Teachers for the Army will they come cannot you send unmarried naval officers or of any other)

While what has been done by Congress during its recent session is not certainly known here, it is feared that action was not taken in the matter of Army instructors for Korea. In case Army officers may not come, I have assumed that other persons from America, competent to drill troops, would be acceptable to Korea; thus it was that I ask in my telegram as to whether naval officers or others might not be selected in lieu of Army officers. Naval Officers of the line, or Marine Officers of the Navy could, in my opinion, serve here satisfactorily. I would suggest that at least three officers are required: one of these should be of mature years and experience, the others, younger men to serve as his assistants.

George C. Foulk

NO. 63.
Department of State
Washington, D. C.
August 19, 1885

Confidential

George C. Foulk, U.S.N.
    Seoul, Korea

Sir:

    I have received through Mr. Richard B. Hubbard, the successor of Mr. John A. Bingham, in the Mission to Japan, a certified copy of your letter to the latter of June 23rd 1885, in respect to the presence in Corea of Mr. Alexis de Speyer, Secretary of the Russian Legation to Japan. Your letter to Mr. Bingham confirms other statements made in your recent despatches to the department, tending to show that Seoul is the center of conflicting and almost hostile intrigues involving the interests of China, Japan, Russia and England, and that it is clearly the interest of the United States to hold aloof from all this and do nothing nor be drawn into anything which would look like taking sides with any of the contestants or entering the lists of intrigue for our own benefit. Hence, the exercise of the utmost discretion on your part is necessary. It may be especially needful for you to let it be distinctly understood that your government in no wise originated or is now disposed to press the proposal to obtain United States Military officers as instructors in Corea. The desire of Corea that such officers should be sent out with the sanction of this government is most friendly and flattering. It cannot, however, be acceded to without the consent of Congress. The urgency of Corea upon the immediate despatch of the officers is almost embarrassing, in view of this fact. At the same time, there is the most abundant evidence that the suggestion of so employing American Army officers is not of the nature of a selfish proposal. The Corean request has been openly addressed to this Government through and supported by the governments of China and Japan, as is apparent from the enclosed copies of notes addressed to the representatives of those friendly powers at this capital.

While entertaining a high opinion of your prudence and ability, in the embarrassing situation of isolation and responsibility in which you now are, and quite willing to permit you to decide for yourself in all ordinary emergencies, yet it is deemed proper to instruct you to communicate without reserve, with the United States Ministers at Peking and Tokio, Mr. Charles Denby and Mr. Hubbard respectively. The three countries, China, Japan, and Corea, bear to the United States a common, almost identical relation in this Corean matter, and the United States can take no action which might even in appearance, seem to favor or oppose the policy of either China or Japan, without impairing the position of friendly impartiality towards all which it is the duty and the pleasure of this nation to maintain. Hence, our representation in those three countries should work as a unit in all that concerns Corea. The large public experience of Mr. Hubbard and Colonel Denby, makes it proper that they should be consulted whenever feasible, and lends weight to their counsels.

In this connection reference is also made to my instruction to you No. 62 of the 19th instant.

T. F. Bayard

3.

ENGLAND, RUSSIA, AND KOREA

NO. 7   *Confidential*   Department of State,
                                       Washington, May 1, 1883

Lucius H. Foote, Esq.,

Sir:

I transmit, herewith, for your information, the enclosed copy of a despatch of February 9th last, marked confidential, from the United States Minister at Peking, touching a reported rumor that Russia proposes negotiating a convention with Corea, independent of the existing stipulations contained in our own with that Kingdom.

                                       Fredk. T. Frelinghuysen

NO. 125.   *Confidential*   Legation of the United States,
                                       Peking, 9th February, 1883.
Secretary of State.

Sir:

In my despatch No. 87, I referred to the fact that the Russian Government had not made a treaty with Corea, and had shown no disposition to follow the example of England, Germany and the United States.

I recently learned in an indirect manner that the Russian foreign office had given orders to a high official in Siberia to proceed to Corea in the spring and negotiate a convention.

The intent of the Russians in doing so is to regulate the trade along the Corean and Siberian frontiers, and perhaps rectify the boundary line in certain parts of Corea to make it more satisfactory to Russia.

I mentioned the rumour in conversation with the Russian *Chargé d'Affaires* Mr. Waeber. In his reply he neither denied nor affirmed it, but left on my mind the impression that Russia did propose a convention of some kind with Corea, and preferred to make it in her own way without the knowledge or the interference of the other powers, this would be in keeping with the general tenor of Russian policy in Asia.

                                       Jno. Russell Young.

NO. 11.   Department of State,
                                              Washington, June 29, 1883

Lucius H. Foote, Esq.,

Sir:

I am in receipt of Mr. Bingham's No. 1688, of the 30th ultimo, touching an article from the Japan Daily Herald of that date, stating that Great Britain and Germany had postponed the ratification of their treaties with Corea, for one year and commenting unfavorably upon the international policy adopted toward that Kingdom by the United States.

I transmit copy of Mr. Bingham's despatch, for your fuller information, and confidentially observe in this connection that it is unofficially learned here that Great Britain and Germany have declined to ratify their treaties and that new ones are to be negotiated, the German Government having requested that the British representative (probably Sir Harry Parkes, Her Majesty's Minister in Japan) should act for Germany as well as for Great Britain in the premises. It is further understood that this request has been acceded to.

Adding that I have communicated information of like import to Mr. Bingham, in response to his despatch,

                                                    John Davis
                                                    Acting Secretary.

NO. 1688   United States Legation,
                                               Tokei, Japan, May 30, 1883.

Secretary of State

Sir,

I am this morning in the receipt of the Japan Daily Herald of last evening the 29th instant which contains a very significant editorial article, a copy of which is herewith to the effect that Mr. Aston, Her Britannic Majesty's Consul at Kobe has just returned from Corea and that owing to the unsatisfactory character of the Corean treaties, Great Britain and Germany have resolved with the assent of the Corean Government to postpone ratifications until the end of the year.

After Great Britain has done her utmost as I have shown in my number 1687 to prevent the ratification of our Treaty with Corea and also to prevent the exchange of the ratification thereof, now comes the Herald with what I regard to be a semi-official announcement as follows. "This rational delay contrasts most favorably with the precipitate action of America in exchanging ratifications and sending General Foote there."

I note not without satisfaction that Great Britain in taking this action alone with Germany seems to ignore all other European States and especially the French Government which it is understood has negotiated a Treaty with Corea. Possibly it is expected that France will await instructions before venturing to ratify or exchange her Treaty with Corea.

The near future will determine whether national advantage will not accrue to the United States from the policy of justice which our government has inaugurated in Corea, not with standing the manifesto of the Herald that "no national advantage is likely to accrue to the United States from the precipitate action of America," as it is termed in the premises.

Jno. A. Bingham.

NO. 23   August 21, 1883, (Seoul)
Secretary of State
Sir:

In a former dispatch No. 4 I mentioned to you that at the instance of Her Brittanic Majesties Representative in Japan, a Mr. Aston had visited Corea upon some special service, I now learn that he came for the purpose of concluding a new treaty; which treaty was signed by himself, without powers, on behalf of the British Government and by one of the under officials of the Foreign Office, on behalf of His Majesty the King of Corea.

The treaty is said to comprise three Articles—
Article 1. sets forth the usual declaration of amity etc.
Article II provides for ex-territorial jurisdiction.
Article III contains the favored nation clause.

It seems to me that by the United action of all Western powers all desirable modifications to the first treaties might have been made.

In Mr. Low's Memorial to Earl Granville, I perceive that objection is urged to the prohibition of Opium. This may account for the strenous opposition to the treaty concluded by Admiral Willes; if so, it is a wicked concession to the selfishness of commerce, which hardly accords with the spirit of the age. At present I believe these people are entirely free from the odious Opium habit. Lucius H. Foote

NO. 37   Confidential   Oct. 30, 1883

Secretary of State

Sir,

Sir Harry Parkes, Her Brittanic Majesty's Envoy to Peking, and Mr. Zappe, H. I. Me. G. Consul General at Yokohama and Commissioner to Corea, have arrived at Seoul, for the purpose of negotiating new treaties with this government. They made their calls yesterday at the Foreign Office, and afterwards upon me. Nothing was said by the German Commissioner regarding the objects of his Mission. Sir Harry made some significant inquiries as to the feeling among Government officials concerning China. I replied to him that I thought there was a divided sentiment upon that subject, but, that the existing relations had been of long duration, and I doubted if their inclinations were sufficiently pronounced to effect in any way their actions. He said that he had had an interview with Li Hung Chang on the eve of his departure from China in which the Vice Roy said, "You are indebted to me for the treaty with Corea, which you have already negotiated, and I suppose you are dissatisfied with it on account of the Opium restriction."

Sir Harry denied emphatically, that his government desired to force Opium upon Corea.

Concerning the receptions accorded by Their Majesties the King and Queen to Mrs. Foote, and the sending of a Corean Embassy to the United States, he said, he feared that the Corean Government was moving too rapidly; I replied, that I supposed it depended somewhat upon the direction in which it moved.

At the conclusion of the interview, I assured him that the Government of the United States would regard with favor any movement on the part of Great Britain and Germany to enter into equitable treaty relations with Corea. He replied that pending the negotiations he should be pleased to confer with me from time to time.

                                        Lucius H. Foote

NO. 66 April 26, 1884

Secretary of State

Sir,

At a private audience at the Palace yesterday, His Majesty, after informing me that H.B.M's Representative Sir Harry Parkes had arrived at the open port of Jenchuan; asked if I thought it would be possible to modify the Treaty lately concluded with Great Britain before the exchange of ratification.

I said to him that such modification would necessarily cause delays, and that unless he considered the proposed changes of vital importance, it would probably be better to exchange the ratifications and trust to future negotiation to rectify any defect.

I then took occasion in compliance with instructions, to extend to him the congratulations of my Government on the conclusion of the treaties. His majesty asked, as he has done upon several occasions, if replies had been received to the requests referred to, in my No. 32, I could only say that, as yet, I was unable to give him the desired information, but hoped to do so soon. He said, "I have read with great pleasure the kindly sentiments expressed by His Excellency the President of the U. States in his late message, and I would ask you to convey to him, my sincere thanks for his explicit and friendly words."

Referring to his relations with neighboring countries, I said, that it was the desire of my Government to see the utmost harmony prevail between the Oriental Nations, and I believed that with moderation and prudence, all international questions which gave uneasiness to His Majesty, would in time be happily determined.

Reiterating his intention to ask advice and counsel as heretofore, the audience terminated.

Lucius H. Foote

NO. 172 May 19, 1885

Secretary of State

Sir:

Upon receipt of news in the East of the strained relations between Russia and England respecting the Afghanistan boundary, it was reported that at once four English vessels of war had proceeded to Port Hamilton, a harbor of an island off the South coast of Korea: Known to Koreans as Komun-to, or Komun Seum. On or about the 11th instant, the Korean Government accepted as a fact the news of there being at Port Hamilton, four English vessels of war, one of which was the "Agamemnon," a heavy iron-clad vessel, pre-eminently intended for harbor or shore defence. This news, I was informed by the President of the Foreign Office, had not been received from Korean sources, but through the reports of western foreigners in Korea.

During a call at the Foreign Office my attention was called to this matter in such a manner as to imply that among a certain number of officials, it was a source of much apprehension and of some indignation against England; these officers claiming that the sending of war ships to Port Hamilton, without obtaining permission of the Korean Government was an unfriendly act in the part of Great Britain and a breach of the treaty made with her by Korea. It was further stated that the matter would be laid before the foreign representatives in Korea, with a view to making a protest against this act of England. A few days later, the President of the Foreign Office called upon me, and while his attitude was somewhat milder, his view of the Port Hamilton matter accorded with that already conveyed to me at the Foreign Office.

On both of these occassions, I stated that while it was right that Korea should exercise vigilance always in maintaining her rights, it seemed to me that under the circumstances, the strong feeling shown by these officers against England was premature and out of place, and that it was certainly not advisable, in view of their evident ignorance of the intentions of England, or even the details of the Port Hamilton affair, to expose such feeling to the English Government.

Recalling the ignorance of Koreans of events of the outside world, and absence of effective means of transmitting information in their own country, it occurred to me that there must be some force at work among them tending to force Korea into partisanship in possible difficulties between England and Russia. Without much doubt, as I have discovered, the attitude above referred to is due to Mr. P. G. Von Mollendorff, the Superintendent of Customs and the practical advisor of the Korean Foreign Office. This officer has stated to me that he had had negotiations with Russia several months ago, and knew with certainty that Russia would not make any occupation of Korean territory, implying certainly, that therefore, the entrance of English ships of war into Port Hamilton must not be meant

England, Russia, and Korea

as a precaution against Russian occupation of that port, or any other near it, and must therefore be looked upon by Koreans as an act demanding explanation upon a rigid call. This officer also told me the Korean government was about to send aboard a German Steamer now plying between Chemulpho and Nagasaki, a Korean officer who by using a powerful telescope, would examine into the conduct of the English ships, as the steamer passed near this port (Hamilton) enroute to Nagasaki.

However, on or about the 14th instant, two Chinese men of war, with Admiral Ting, arrived at Masanphō near Chemulpho, bringing a Chinese Officer of rank, who at once came to Seoul. On or about the 16th, Mr. Von Mollendorff and a Korean Vice President of the Foreign Office sailed in one of the Chinese vessels of war, to visit Port Hamilton. To this effect I have been informed by the President of the Foreign Office.

The Japanese representative has called to see me with reference to "armed occupation", as he termed it, of Port Hamilton by England. He had been approached on the subject by the President of the Foreign Office, and at first seemed disposed to adopt his views, believing the influence of the foreign representatives in combined action necessary in the case; in this view I beleived it discreet to give him no encouragement at the time, nor have I since.

The German representative has but little to say on the subject. Incidentally I referred to the subject in conversation with the Acting Consul General for England, who had evidently no idea of the feeling in the Korean Foreign Office on it, nor had been spoken to at all of it. I feel assured from his remarks that the entry of the English ships into Port Hamilton, was believed by him to be what was deemed a necessary precaution by the English Government in view of the outbreak of a great war with Russia, and not at all meant to be a permanent occupation. However, as represented by Kim Yun Sik, the President of the Foreign Office, who was present at a discussion in China upon the subject of a treaty between England and Korea, three years ago, at that time, the English representative made certain overtures respecting the lease or cession of Port Hamilton to his government; and similar interest of England in Port Hamilton was shown in the more recent treaty negociations between England and Korea.

It would seem particularly unfortunate that such a question should have sprung up, with the attendent circumstances as herein narrated,—at this time, immediately following the close of the conference at Peking, the tenor of the issues which seem to admit of greater independence for Korea, and freedom from the self-imposed interference of China or Japan—more especially the former. It is very probable that the jealousy of Japan will be aroused afresh by this assistance rendered Korea by China in examining Port Hamilton by Chinese vessels-of war bearing Korean Officials. It is impossible to say with exactness how the Chinese were thus brought into the matter, but the evidences apparent are to the effect that they appeared voluntarily, or were called by the influence for China which remains in the Korean Government; this influence is exerted it may safely be said, by M. P. G. Mollendorff and the President of the Foreign Office—who is readily subservient to him, and the Chinese representative in Seoul. It is worthy of remark that the great body of Korean nobles and other officers show no interest whatever in the affair of Port Hamilton.

It would seem that the King and truly Korean Government is unable to dislodge the influence for China centered in the Korean Foreign Office, or even divide it without competent Western assistants in its service, and these it cannot promptly obtain. And yet that the King and nobles are all powerful in Korea, irrespective of the small Chinese faction represented by the officers herein named, all my experiences in this country point to unmistakeably.

George C. Foulk

NO. 174　　　　　　　　　　　　　　　　　　　　　　　　　　May 25, 1885.

Secretary of State

Sir:

Referring to my despatch No. 173, dated May 21st instant, I have to report further on the same subject, that on yesterday, the Chinese Admiral Ting, with the Koreans sent to visit Port Hamilton, returned to Seoul. This morning, Admiral Ting called upon me and frankly described his visit to Port Hamilton. He found there, six English vessels of war and two merchant steamers with coal; an English Ensign had been raised on the island.

In reply to questions, the English senior Commanding Officer could only state that he had been stationed there by his Admiral. Admiral Ting then went to Nagasaki where he interviewed the English Admiral in regard to the occupation of Port Hamilton: he was informed that the temporary occupation had been ordered by the Home Government. Admiral Ting further stated that he inferred the English ships would speedily be withdrawn, now that peace was quite assured between England and Russia.

The tenor of the Admiral's remarks was highly gratifying to me as corroborating in every particular the views I had formed on the subject, and had communicated to the Korean Government in reply to its repeated earnest (~~appeals~~) requests for advice and explanation. The indications now point to reassurance on the part of the Koreans and an end to the difficulty which unquestionably arose among them through bad advice and misrepresentation.

George C. Foulk

NO. 180.   June 16, 1885.

Secretary of State

Sir:

I have to inform you that the Secretary of the Russian Legation in Tokio, Japan, Mr. Alexis de Speyer, has taken up his residence in Seoul under the title "Agent Provisoire" for Russia.

This officer has informed me that his duty pertains to the occupation of Port Hamilton by England and that in case the port is by either negociation or force, allowed to be retained by England, he bears instructions directed towards effecting the (~~permanent maintainance~~) acquirement—to use his own (~~words~~) language "of ten times as much territory" by Russia, from Korea.

The seizure of the port is regarded as a hostile act of England against Russia, and may be the cause of augmenting the difficulties arising between England and Russia out of the Afghan boundary question.

While the English authorities in the East have been maintaining that the occupation of Port Hamilton is but temporary, the extent of the work being done there by the Naval Force gives rise to the very general opinion that words are being played upon in these expressions, and the permanent maintenance of the port is being aimed at by England.

The Commanding Officer of a Japanese man-of-war, who has just returned to Chemulpho from an inspection of the Port Hamilton group informs me, that on June 3, there were nine English vessels of war and two transports there. Lines of booms had been prepared, torpedos numerously laid, and the approaches to the harbor obstructed by stone piles; observation island of the group was patrolled by sentries and a torpedo house built upon it; other houses and a jetty were in course of construction. 300 Korean laborers had been impressed and were busily at work with the men of the fleet. A Japanese man-of-war had recently narrowly escaped striking torpedos near the islands.

It has been asserted that China permitted England to occupy Port Hamilton. The representatives of Asiatic Countries here, however, indignantly deny this and unanimously denounce the conduct of England in the strongest terms.

George C. Foulk

NO. 59   Department of State,
Washington, August 18, 1885.

Ensign George C. Foulk, U.S.N.

Sir:–

I have received and read with interest your confidential despatch No. 186 of June 23rd last, in regard to the secret negotiations of Mr. P. G. von Möllendorff, for Corea, with Russia.

In this connection, I desire to advert to the conclusion of your despatch suggesting that the Chinese and Japanese troops should remain longer in Corea, and to remind you that very great discretion is necessary in making such intimations to the Chinese and Japanese representatives. The Government of the United States has no concern in these matters beyond that of a friendly State which has treated with Corean as independent and sovereign and hopes to see her position as such among nations assured.

T. F. Bayard

NO. 187   *Confidential*   June 26, 1885

Secretary of State

Sir:

I have the honor to transmit herewith a copy of translation of a letter addressed me by the President of the Office for Foreign Affairs of Korea, relating to the British occupation of Port Hamilton.

It is very probable that this second appeal to the foreign representatives is in consequence of the attitude shown by the Russian Agent Provisoire, and meant to convince him of the sincerity of the intentions of Korea to resist any attempt on the part of England to hold Port Hamilton.

The English Consul General in Seoul has expressed to me his belief that England will relinquish Port Hamilton when it understands that the negociations it suspected of having been carried on between Russia and Korea— per Mr. Von Möllendorff were not authorized by the Korean government.

George C. Foulk

NO. 188 *Confidential* June 26, 1885

Secretary of State

Sir:

I have the honor to enclose herewith, a copy of translation of minutes of a discussion at the Korean Foreign Office between the President of the Office, for Korea, and Mr. Alexis de Speyer, "Agent Provisoire" for Russia to Korea.

The copy from which the translation was prepared was sent me privately, for inspection, by His Majesty the King.

In connection with the matter presented in the translation, I may state that the arrival of a Russian Ambassador to exchange the ratified treaties of Korea and Russia, has been for some time expected. M. de Speyer has informed me that he would remain here until this Ambassador shall have arrived.

George C. Foulk

NO. 189 June 29, 1885.

Secretary of State

Sir:

Since addressing my despatch No. 187, dated June 26th, I have received a communication from the office for Foreign Affairs of Korea supplementry to that of which a copy was transmitted with despatch No. 187, in which the good offices of the United States Government, as in mediation, are asked for by the Korean Government, under Article 1, of the treaty between Korea and the United States, to effect the release of Port Hamilton now occupied by a British Naval Force acting under the orders of the home government of Great Britain.

In this protest, the Korean government makes no distinction between the temporary and the permanent occupation.

George C. Foulk

NO. 191 July 3, 1885

Secretary of State

Sir:

I have the honor to transmit herewith a copy of translation of a memorandum of conversation between Kim, the President of the Korean Foreign Office, and M. de Speyer, the Russian Agent in Seoul, on June 20 ultimo.

As shown by the memorandum itself, this conversation took place before M. de Speyer's audience at the Palace referred to in my despatch No. 186. This memorandum like that transmitted with my No. 188, was prepared in the Foreign Office for his Majesty's inspection. A copy of it was not voluntarily shown me by the Koreans, and that from which the enclosed translation was made was obtained through the Japanese Legation.

I shall endeavor to procure a copy of the letter of M. de Speyer—translated by M. Von Mollendorff—referred to in the memorandum herewith transmitted; with this, the record of M. de Speyer's negociations here will be complete.

M. de Speyer is yet in Seoul, and it is intimated from His Majesty that in view of his having no credentials, his proposals will be left standing for discussion when the Russian Minister shall have arrived.

George C. Foulk

NO. 192. Confidential July 5, 1885

Secretary of State

Sir:

I beg to enclose herewith a copy of memorandum of a conversation between Kim, President of the Korean Foreign Office, and M. de Speyer, Russian Agent in Seoul, on July 2d inst.

It is now understood that the conversation reported in the memorandum above referred to closes for the present M. de Speyer's negociations with the Korean Government.

On yesterday, M. de Speyer called upon me, and after announcing that he was about to return to Japan, gave me the following account of his object in visiting Korea, stating that he desired to explain this and his work here to preclude any erroneous opinions which might be formed from the accounts given by (opinions of) others.

In February last, the Korean Ambassador sent to Japan in consequence of the revolutionary troubles of December last, and Mr. Von Möllendorff, who held the office of Vice Ambassador, came to the Russian Legation, and after stating that the Japanese troops and Chinese troops were to be withdrawn from Korea, added that it was the intention of His Majesty, the King of Korea to ask for Russian Drill instructors for the Korean troops; would Russia comply to this request? In reply, the Russian Minister stated that he could but refer the matter to his sovereign; this he was requested to do, by the Korean Ambassador.

Accordingly the matter was presented to the Russian Government by telegraph and a favourable reply was duly received, but not until the Ambassadors had returned to Korea.

In May last, Mr. Von Möllendorff visited Nagasaki, Japan, as representative of the Korean Government, to confer with the English Admiral upon the occupation of Port Hamilton. His presence there having become known to the Russian Minister in Tokio, by telegraphic message, through the Russian Consul at Nagasaki, he was informed that Russia was prepared to send military instructors to Korea.

The Russian Minister knew nothing of the affairs of the Korean government, nor was he aware that the United States had been asked by Korea to furnish military instructors. As Mr. Von Möllendorf held a title of nobility under the Korean government, was a Vice President of the Foreign Office, and then serving as special Ambassador, he was believed in the matter of these military instructors, to be acting by authority of the King and Government of Korea.

In June last, M. de Speyer was directed to proceed to Korea and complete arrangements for the reception and service of the Russian military instructors. He came here, believing that he was expected—that the King and general government of Korea were fully aware of the arrangements entered into by Mr. Von Möllendorff.

Upon arriving here, as usual with all persons coming to deal with Korea, he found great difficulty through language and ignorance of the government, in seeking communications, through Koreans: therefore, for some ten days, he dealt with Mr. Von Möllendorff solely, as the representative, by authority, of the Korean government.

The work of M. de Speyer with the King and real government of Korea is clearly shown in the copies of memoranda of conversations at the Foreign Office and the despatches from this Legation.

M. de Speyer has informed me, however, that he has not addressed any communication to the Korean government in writing.

M. de Speyer states that he now is aware that the subject of employing Russian Officers in Korea was originated and negociated upon by Mr. Von Möllendorff wholly without authority, and wholly unknown to any Korean native official. At the same time, he states that as this subject is one which has been brought to the attention of his Sovereign, and has been acted upon by His Majesty, the Emperor of Russia, it is with strong feelings of deep embarrassment that he contemplates reporting to his government the turn affairs have taken; and he ventures to express the opinion that Russia may force Korea to accept the Russian Officers. M. de Speyer states that in all probability, the Russian Minister will duly arrive to exchange the treaty ratifications.

Unquestionably, Mr. Von Möllendorff has assumed without authority, the Sovereign's and governmentel right to make those negociations with Russia. The whole matter being now exposed he is denounced by Koreans, Chinese and Japanese in strong terms and must certainly leave the service of Korea. The English representative here has made a strong protest against his having a part in the government of Korea on the ground that he has acted treacherously against Korea and for Russia: his protest has had strong effect upon the Korean officials.

M. de Speyer has not told me of any other subject than that of the employment of military officers of Russia, upon which he negociated with Mr. Von Möllendorff. It is not however, unlikely but that graver (questions) matters were broached, if not vigorously acted upon in these negociations. It may be said, however, that the general effect of the negociations was towards establishing Korea as the protectorate of Russia; ulterior objects to this can at present only be surmised.

I would respectfully and earnestly beg the attention of the Department of State to those parts of the correspondence on this subject, which pertain to the employment of American assistants in Korea. As it now stands, it would seem that Korea must accept only Russian Officers should the United States not speedily take some action upon the requests made it by His Majesty, the King. Russian Officers could only be accepted here and serve harmoniously under well understood guarantee of the neutrality of Korea given by the various powers whose interests are drawn towards her. The salaries proposed long since to be given to the chief assistants asked from the United States—are

Adviser—at least 5200 Mexican dollars
Senior Military Officer—5000 dollars.
Junior Military Officer—3500 dollars.

George C. Foulk

NO. 196 July 6, 1885

Secretary of State,

Sir:

Referring to my despatches Nos. 187, June 26, 1885, and 189, June 29, 1885, I beg to state that the Government of Korea, on yesterday, recalled the letter asking for mediation and assistance referred to therein, in regard to the English occupation of Port Hamilton. I learn this was done at the request of the Consul General for England here, who will discuss the matter further with the Korean government.

George C. Foulk

NO. 223.   *Confidential*   Sept. 1, 1885.

Secretary of State

Sir,

I have the honor to report that a despatch has been received by the Korean Government from Mr. O'Connor, the British Chargé d'Affaires, ad. interim, at Peking in reply to the letters of protest addressed him by the President of the Office for Foreign Affairs of Korea against the occupation of Port Hamilton by England.

These letters of protest were despatched in May last, and copies of translations giving their substance, were transmitted to the Department of State with my despatch No. 173, dated May 21st, 1885.

In his despatch, after referring to the impracticability of communicating the wishes of the Korean Government to the British Home Government by telegraph, Mr. O'Connor proceeds to say that it gave him much satisfaction to learn that the appeal for mediation in the matter of Port Hamilton by the Korean Government to the other treaty powers had been withdrawn: had this not been done, it is possible that only unnecessary complications and difficulties would have been engendered. Mr. O'Connor states that he may assure His Excellency, the President of the Foreign Office that England will fully respect the integrity of Korea and the dignity of His Majesty, and will do nothing in regard to Port Hamilton, which may be productive of difficulty to Korea.

In reply to the charge that England had abruptly seized the Port Hamilton group without previous or suitable explanation having been made to Korea, Mr. O'Connor's despatch says that it was imperative for England at the time to assume the guard of the islands: and to show that England respected the rights of Korea, instructions were issued at the same time to the Consul General in Seoul to confer with the Korean Government with the view of making an arrangement by which Korea would receive satisfaction—as by fair material compensation for the lease of the islands. When the difficulties, based upon which the temporary occupation was made, shall have passed, further and more satisfactory negotiations in regard to the matter will be entered into with Korea.

I have in the above given in my own language for the most part the substance of Mr. O'Connor's (letter) despatch. Its tone was excellent, though mildly guarded in expression in parts, and its effect has been to give some assurance to the Korean Government. The most pleasing features of it are the statement that the integrity of Korea and the dignity of His Majesty, the King, will be fully respected, and the use of the word "temporary", wherever the occupation is referred to.

In explanation of my being aware of the substance of this despatch, I may say that I have read the Original of it: there had been made an error in the translation which accompanied it, and in the absence of any person in the Government who could clearly understand the meaning intended, I was asked to translate, and in this was shown, the despatch and translation.

In connection with this subject I may state that I have learned that during the past month the English Consul General has approached the Korean Government with the view of its acceptance of lease money for Port Hamilton, the sum of $20000. per year having been suggested. The Government thus far, however, persists in its refusal to acknowledge the lease or submit to the occupation on any terms.

At the time of addressing the Department my No. 172, dated May 19th, no ensigns were known to have been raised over the Port Hamilton Group, but that the English fleet lay quietly in the harbor having little or no communication with the shore. The report would seem quite accurate that the English ensigns were hoisted on the several islands suddenly upon the approach of a Russian vessel of war, on or about April 28th, after the fleet had remained inactive in the harbor, about three weeks. A number of English men-of-war yet remain at Port Hamilton at all times, and despatch vessels are actively plying thence to Nagasaki, Tientsin and Chemulpho, making round trips. The English Admiral recently endeavored to have a Japanese steamer plying between Nagasaki and Chemulpho, bring supplies to Port Hamilton, but the Japanese government promptly forbade the steamer to touch there.

The English Naval authorities some time since laid a line of submarine telegraph from Port Hamilton to Gutzlaff Island off Shanghai, where it joins the main line on the Chinese coast.

George C. Foulk

NO. 238　　　　　　　　　　　　　　　　　　　　　　　　Oct. 14, 1885

Secretary of State

Sir:

I have the honor to report that Mr. I. Waeber, chargé d'affairs for Russia has arrived and taken up his residence temporarily in Seoul. He came on board a Russian vessel of war which arrived at Chemulpho on the 3rd instant.

I have learned that Mr. Waeber comes for the purpose of exchanging the ratifications of the treaty negotiated with Korea last year; however he has entered into new negotiations with the Korean Government with the view of securing under the treaty the right of overland trade for Russia with Korea, to effect which the opening for trade with the Russia of a trading post on the northeast boundary of Korea is requested.

The position of the proposed trading post desired by Russia is on the Tumen River at some distance from the sea and as thus is probably placed to be the equivalent of the trading post of China and Korea at Ichow (Oichū—in Korean) on the Yalu River the boundary between China and Korea.

At present the disposition of the government towards Mr. Waeber's proposition is guardedly favorable; however, in case a trading post is to be established, the government proposes as its site one of three places on the east coast of Korea a little to the southward of the mouth of the Tumen River, the nearest one to Possiette, the southernmost Russian town of Eastern Siberia, being about 130 miles by the sea route distant.

Along the northeastern border of Korea Russia and China are contiguous. A question as to the boundary separating them here has sprung up and commissions have been sent by the respective governments to settle the dispute by fixing the boundary line. Russia claims that the boundary maintained by China is placed too far to the eastward. This question has much bearing upon Mr. Waeber's negotiations in regard to the trading post for Korea and Russia.

Mr. Waeber's manner of dealing with the Korean government is mild and very satisfactory to it; the attitude displayed by M. de Speyer as some time ago reported to the Department had given rise to apprehension on the part of the Korean government, of difficulty in negotiating with the Russian representative who was to follow him.

In his call upon me Mr. Waeber touched upon M. de Speyer's work in his conversation remarking that that officer, being a young man, had assumed unwarranted authority in his manner of conducting it.

George C. Foulk

England, Russia, and Korea

NO. 272 Confidential January 18, 1886

Secretary of State

Sir:

I have the honor to report that recently there have been further conferences between the President of the Korean Office of Foreign Affairs and the British Consul General in regard to Port Hamilton Islands. These have been conducted with much caution and secrecy and I have been unable to ascertain details; however I believe that no definite conclusion has been reached as to the future action of England with regard to the group. For several weeks past now dispatche boats of the English Navy have been lying at Chemulpho daily expecting dispatches to be carried to Port Hamilton, and to Chefoo—for Peking.

I am certainly aware that upon the receipt of news, some time since, that an armed expedition had sailed from Japan for Korea under Kim Ok Kiun, upon which occasion three Chinese and two English vessels of war quickly proceeded to Chemulpho, one of the latter from Port Hamilton, the British Consul General took some pains to impress upon the Chinese representative the advantage of having an English Naval force stationed so advantageously as at Port Hamilton.

It is quite an established fact that the Korean Customs Service, under Mr. H. F. Merrill, an American who was placed in charge peremptorily by China, is regarded by the Chinese and English authorities as a branch of the Customs of China, the head of which, Sir Robert Heart, is most actively engaged in political affairs of China and England. The most cordial relations are being maintained here between the head of the Customs, Mr. Merrill, the Chinese representative Yuen, and the British Consul General, Mr. Baber; the general line of conduct and speech of these officials would prompt the inference that they are disposed to ignore entirely the independent action of the Korean Government, and to support the ruling of China in all matters of importance pertaining to Korea.

The general result of my observations tends to the belief that England is desirous of operating on Korea to acquire the Port Hamilton group, through China's distrust of Russia, and with this view gives the necessary support to China's pretensions to rule in Korea. His Majesty still refuses to sanction the ceding of Port Hamilton. As to the views of the Korean Government, as represented by the Foreign Office, on this point, I am unable to report, but there are evidences that the work of the Foreign Office is more fully reported by it to the Chinese representative than to His Majesty and the Ministerial Cabinet.

The question as to the powers and title of the Chinese representative, as reported in my No. 255, of Nov. 25, 1885, remains open. I am not aware that any of the foreign representatives have acknowledged Mr. Yuen to be "Resident," however, that it remains the intention of Mr. Yuen to be Resident in the full sense of the word as in title of governmental policy, there can be no doubt. While the officers of the Korean Government are in ignorance of the significance of this English title, many of them, quite apart from considerations of His Majesty's wishes and views, do yield practically, in the high position of authority they yield to Mr. Yuen, the attributes of Resident as we understand it, to him.

Mr. Waeber, the chargé d'affairs of Russia has again opened work with the Foreign Office in regard to the establishment of a Russo-Korean trading post on the Tumen River. He will probably insist that the site shall be inland, on the Tumen River at some distance from the sea. He has expressed to me his dissatisfaction with the tendencies of the Korean Government in sending officers, as was promised, to prepare maps of the Tumen country with the view of determining the State site of the trading post. The opposition to the establishment of the post is confined to the Chinese and their faction in the Korean Government who lay stress upon the fact that the Russian authorities of Southern Primorskaya have rendered much assistance to a considerable number of Koreans in past years who crossed from their own country into Russian territory. Repeatedly Korea has asked that these people be returned from Siberia. The Russian authorities claim the Koreans (estimated at from 20–40,000) came into their territory voluntarily having been driven by starvation and the tyrannical cruelty of the Tai Wen Kun; and that they begged to be allowed to settle on unoccupied land of Russia. Both China and England show great watchfulness of Mr. Waeber's work.

The Korean Government has recently secured a loan of $100,000 from the German house of Meyer and Co., at Chemulpho, at 10% interest. The only other foreign debt of the government on account of loans is one of taels 200000, at 8%, loaned by the Chinese Government practically, through the China Merchant Steam Navigation Company.

I may add in regard to the money affairs of Korea, that little or none of the general revenues of Korea, as derived under the Korean systems purely, has been used to defray expenses incurred through the Government as represented by the Foreign Office. All such revenues are held in the King's name, and certainly no considerable part of it has ever been placed at the disposition of the government for paying foreign expenses. A part of the Customs revenue only would seem to have fallen for disbursement to the Foreign Office. The policy of his Majesty to direct personally the disposition of his revenues has certainly proved a wise one in the light of the experiences of the past three years, though it must certainly be disapproved of by the Chinese whose authority does not seem effective beyond the Foreign Office.

On the above understanding of the money affairs of Korea, I have been careful to encourage only those expenditures to Americans as were assuredly approved of and authorized by His Majesty personally.

George C. Foulk

NO. 24.	Confidential	Legation of the U. S. Söul, Korea
Secretary of State		August 4, 1886

Sir:

Mr. Waeber, Russian Chargé D'Affaires—in Söul, is making application to the Foreign Office to have established a Trading Post in Korea 100 ri (about 35 mi.) from the Russian border of the N.E. province and also to assent to Russian soldiers, armed, &c., travelling freely to the post.

This request has not yet been formally considered, but I am advised will not be granted. The advisers of the govt. suggest that the most that can be given to Russia is a Trading Post on the border to correspond to Aichu (Ichu) on the Yalu river—the trading border post of China & Korea which is accessable to light draught vessels from the sea & by the favored nation clause open to all powers in treaty with Korea.

The Dept. is no doubt aware of the fact that the Russians have made Vladivostok their chief naval station on the Pacific—this port, however, in latitude 43° is closed by the ice for three months of the year & it is feared by some here that Russia is looking to obtaining possession of Port Lazaret in lat. 39° on Broughton Bay (the seizure of Port Hamilton by Great Britain having established a precedent).

I think this very probable and would bring them within 115 miles of Söul & Chemulpho.

In the case of war between Russia & China, Russia would undoubtedly seize upon Korea—a single regiment could do the work—and then make Chemulpho the base of operations against Peking—the possession of Korea, then, by any other power could not be permitted by China as it is necessary to the safety of its capital, and I should suppose the Monroe Doctrine would apply?

Of course Great Britain would interfere as she could not permit her enormous China trade to be interrupted, but it would look somewhat as though Mr. Waeber's request was tending to a further step in this direction—ie. to the ultimate possession of Port Lazaret.

Mr. Youen, Chinese Minister, with whom I am on very good terms informs me that the Chinese Squadron is now on the east coast of Korea in the neighborhood of Gensan (Wonshan)!

Wm. H. Parker

NO. 6.   *Confidential*   September 24, 1886

Secretary of State

Sir:

In despatches of this Legation, No. 238, Oct. 14, 1885, and No. 24, Aug. 4, 1886, reference is made to negotiations originated by Russia to effect the establishment of a Russ-Korean Trading Post on or near the border of Korea and the Sea Coast Province of Siberia. I have now to report that recently the Russian Chargé D'Affaires, Mr. S. Waeber, has been actively pressing the Korean government to secure a treaty by which Russia's proposition may be acceded to. A synopsis of the treaty proposed has been shown me by direction of His Majesty the King of Korea. It provides for the establishment of a belt of land 100 *ri* wide (abt. 35 mi. wide) in the territory of each country measuring from the border—the River Tumen— in which trade shall be absolutely free for Koreans and Russians, officers to superintend trade are to be appointed. In addition to the present open ports of Korea, the place Pinyöng, in the north-east Province of Korea— situated by Korean maps, 200 *ri* (about 75 miles) from the Tumen River, is to be open to the trade and residence of Russians after the manner of the other treaty ports of Korea. At this place, Pinyöng, a Russian Consulate is to be established. Until a regularly appointed Consul is sent to Pinyöng, the Governor of South Primorskaya, or any other local Russian officer may serve as Acting Consul. Korea is to establish post-houses for Russian couriers

England, Russia, and Korea 91

across the 100 *ri* belt. Goods coming to Pinyöng on which duty has once been paid at a Korean Treaty Port are duty free. Goods destined for Pinyöng are not to be sold en route from Siberia and are to go by but one route—through Kyöng Hung; at Pinyöng, Customs officials are to examine goods, collect duties, & c. No duties must be leveed on Korean goods coming to Pinyöng. Goods may be removed to other Korean Ports without duty during thirteen months. The treaty stipulates that those Koreans who went to reside in Siberia (said to number from 20–40,000) before 1884—when Russia made her present treaty with Korea, shall be regarded as Russian subjects. No provision for extradition of criminals &c. is made. I add a sketch map to illustrate the treaty and its effects.

In reply to inquiries addressed me by the King and Government, confidentially, with regard to the treaty proposed, I have explained my personal understanding of the effects of yielding to such a treaty, as it is accepted by Korea that a post or place will have to be open to Russia, I have suggested that in the counter propositions Korea might make to Russia, that the free trade belt be excluded; that as a first proposition as to the site of the place to be opened to Russia, some port on the Japan Sea, at some distance from the Tumen River be proposed by Korea instead of Pinyöng; failing in that, a place on the Tumen River, as near its mouth as possible to be proposed. In general, Korea should endeavor to open a port near the Russian border in the same manner as ports have already been opened to the treaty powers, and at most, a strong stand might be made against yielding more with regard to the port than China enjoys in her trading post at Wijü (Ichow)—near the mouth of the Yalu River—the boundary of China and Korea.

Until a few years ago, there was a belt of such "no-man's land" as is proposed in the Russian Treaty, lying between China and Korea. This belt China has absorbed and the Yalu River is her common border with Korea; about 70 miles from the mouth of this River is Ichow (or Wijü) in Korea, which is open to Chinese trade. It is commonly reported that the trade of Ichow is prosperous and increasing.

Near the source of the Tumen River there has been some doubt as to which of the source-tributaries forms the boundary between China and Korea. Within the past year, Chinese have settled beyond the northern tributary or what Korea timidly contended is Korean territory. All the northern boundaries of Korea, while they are generally known to be well defined by nature, are very little known to others at most than Chinese and Russians. Of what has been transpiring along them little is known but I surmise that events of importance have occurred there.

The suggestion would seem pertinent that Russia in her treatment of Korea, is for the purpose of defeating China's pretentions with regard to Korea—if nothing more—simulating her moves in Korea to those made by China. The ultimate effect of the Treaty proposed by Russia to Korea would be to advance the border of Russia at least 100 *ri* into Korea beyond the Tumen River. The conditions under which Pinyöng is proposed to be open would cause the belt of land between that place and the Siberian border—a distance of 200 *ri* (77 miles) to appear as so much open sea. This belt or the one 100 ri wide proposed to be open to free trade, could become at once the home of the 20-40,000 Koreans to be made Russian subjects by the Treaty, and it would be a fait accompli that that area of territory had passed under the rule of Russia.

Pinyöng, once open to Russia as proposed, a road well adapted to military use would soon follow from Russian territory—with Vladivostok as a starting point—down towards Port Lazareff—along the Korean Coast. It is not known that any good harbors exist along this remote part of the coast of Korea, but it is reasonable to suppose nevertheless, that via Pinyöng—which is but twenty-four miles from the coast, Russia would have a useful opening either way to Vladivostok in case that intricate and half closed harbor were blockaded in time of war.

China and England are vigilantly watching Russia. I have reason to believe their representatives here are assisting Korea to frame counter-propositions to Mr. Waeber's treaty. Remark has been made to the effect that England may propose to Korea the opening of Port Hamilton and two other places of Korea—on the northwest coast, one of which is Yung Heung, close to Port Lazareff.

The King and Government of Korea have indicated that Korea can only grant to Russia the opening of a port on the Seacoast or Tumen River, and must insist upon the treaty's including provisions for extradition of fugitives from Justice and suspicious persons. It is proposed that all Koreans in Siberia be sent back to their country.

Judge Denny is yet in China and the result of his work there is not known. His presence is greatly needed in these negotiations with Russia, and the Koreans are endeavoring to postpone action until he shall have returned.

George C. Foulk

4.

CHINA, JAPAN, AND THE STRUGGLE FOR CONTROL OF KOREA

NO. 18. July 19, 1883

Secretary of State

Sir,

It is reported that His Majesty has received an intimation that the Government of China contemplates liberating the Taiwun Kun, with permission to return to Corea. The Taiwun Kun is the adopted father of the King, and was regent during the troubles last year. He is the leader of the party, antagonistic to the new order of things and is bitterly opposed to foreigners. What the effect of his liberation will be, it is difficult to determine. There is no doubt that the Government of Corea fears the consequences, and it may be that it is merely an intimidation on the part of China. In this connection I would say that by the last mail, I received a letter from our Admiral commanding the Asiatic Squadron saying that he desired to send the U.S.S. "Monocacy" on some special service to China; She has already left here, as I have informed you, having on board the Embassy from Corea to the United States. It seems to me prudent that one of our vessels of war should at least for the present, be stationed here; and I have reason to know that this Government earnestly desires it.

Lucius H. Foote

NO. 104 *Confidential* Sept. 2, 1884.

Secretary of State

Sir,

Great interest is manifested by the King and his Ministers in regard to the war now threatening between France and China, and many questions are asked as to its probable effect. The anxiety manifested seems to pertain more particularly to the safety and integrity of their country. There is, however, a division of sentiment. One party contending that China is entitled to their sympathy because she has befriended Corea in the past, and the other secretly hoping that she may be humbled, that thereby her pretensions with reference to neighboring States may be relinquished. The hope is also freely expressed that the war may force China to withdraw her troops stationed here. Fortified as Corea is, by the Treaties lately concluded here, it has seemed to me that China would, in time, voluntarily relinquish her claim to suzerainty; that this is the earnest desire of the King and His people there is no doubt.

Lucius H. Foote

127

Seoul, Corea
December 5, 1884

Secretary of State

Sir:

We are at this moment in the midst of a political revolution. It was inaugurated last evening by the attempted assassination of Min Yong Ik, lately one of the envoys to the United States. It occurred at a dinner party, which was being given by Hong Yeng Shik, vice minister of the embassy to the United States. There were present Pak Yong Hio, brother-in-law to the King; Kim Hong Chip, president of the Corean foreign office; Kim Ok Kinn, vice-president; Von Mollendorf, superintendent of customs; myself, my secretary and interpreter; W. G. Aston, Esq., Her Britannic Majesty's consul-general; Chen Sher Tang, Chinese commissioner; the Japanese secretary of Legation and several other minor officials. As the dinner drew to a close an alarm of fire was given, and nearly all of the guests withdrew from the table and went out of doors or to the windows to view the fire, which seemed near at hand. Perceiving no immediate danger, I returned, with the President of the Corean Foreign Office and several others, to the table. A moment thereafter Min Yong Ik entered the room, his face and clothing covered with blood, which was streaming from seven or eight ghastly wounds. The utmost consternation ensued; The Corean officials divesting themselves of their official robes as they ran, rushed to the courtyard, which was already half filled with soldiers and servants. At this moment a shot was fired, and the entire crowd precipitated themselves over the rear walls and disappeared. Upon the entrance of Min Yong Ik I had gone forward and aided by Von Mollendorf, had placed him in an easy position. I asked that Dr. Allen, an American physician, be sent for, which was done, and leaving the wounded man in charge of Mr. Von Mollendorf, I returned with Mr. Scudder and my interpreter to the legation.

At this moment it is difficult to determine whether the attempted assas-

Struggle for Control 97

sination is the result of some personal feud or whether it has a political signification. All sorts of rumors are afloat. The latest is that the deed was done by a party of students from one of the southern provinces who were enraged at some reforms which Min Yong Ik had instituted since his return from the United States. I shall be enabled to give you more definite information within a few days.

Lucius H. Foote

NO. 128 Legation of the United States
Seoul, Corea, December 17, 1884
Secretary of State

Sir:

We are in the midst of great excitement and, I may say, danger. It seems that the entire movement is an attempted revolution, concocted by a few ill advised young men, under the leadership of Kim Ok Kinn, vice president of the Corean foreign office; Hong Heng Shik, postmaster-general, and Pak Yong Hio, brother-in-law of the King.

Ostensibly dissatisfied with the non-progressive spirit manifested by the leading officials, they determined to seize the Government, obtain control of the person of the King, and to administer public affairs for their own purposes. The first move in their plot was the attempted assassination of Min Yong Ik, and during the excitement occasioned thereby, they rushed to the palace, informed the King that he was in great danger, and persuaded him to move to a smaller palace. The King, fearing perhaps that some great public commotion was taking place, sent messengers to the Japanese legation asking the Minister to come to the palace with his guard of soldiers. After three messages of this kind, the minister consented, and went to the palace, the Japanese soldiers, two hundred in number, being stationed at the gates. In the meantime five of the leading officials of the Government were called to the palace, ostensibly by direction of the King, and while there were put to death. These things occurred on the night of the 4th and the morning of the 5th instant.

About 12 o'clock on the night of the 4th messengers came to me from the King, asking me to come to the palace with my wife and suite, saying that he feared somewhat for our safety, and felt that we would be more secure with him.

The same messengers with the same messages were sent to Mr. Aston, Her Brittanic Majesty's consul-general and to Captain Zembsch, His Imperial German Majesty's commissioner, shortly after. Mr. Aston, his wife and assistant, came to the United States legation with the intention of going to the palace. I told him that upon consideration I had determined not to leave the legation; that I would wait upon his Majesty in the morning to learn his wishes, but that in the uncertainty of affairs I should rely upon the inviolability of the legation, making such preparations for defense as I could. On the morning of the 5th, with her Brittanic Majesty's consul-general, Mr. Aston, and His Imperial German Majesty's commissioner, Captain Zembsch, I went to the small palace occupied by the King. We found crowds of excited people in the streets. Corean soldiers were massed around the entrance, outside; within, Japanese soldiers were guarding the gateways. In the palace I saw the leading revolutionists, who had been installed in the positions made vacant by the death of the high officials. I also met the Japanese minister and his secretary of legation. The King had little to say, and seemed to be in a state of great excitement. After some unimportant conversation we retired.

Immediately after this I called a conference of the representatives, endeavoring to secure the attendance of the Japanese minister, but could not reach him. We jointly consuled the Chinese commissioner to do nothing to disturb the peace or to excite the populace, and under all circumstances to avoid a conflict between Japanese and Chinese troops. He seemed to sanction this line of policy.

During the day, by my advice, the two Americans residing with their families in Seoul came to the Legation. That night the King, accompanied by the Japanese guard, returned to the palace proper.

From sundown until morning crowds of excited people were surging through the streets, but no actual outbreak occurred. Her Britannic Majesty's consul-general, Mr. Aston, his wife, one attaché and servants, came to the legation on the night of the 4th, and remained, by my invitation, for several days.

As before stated, I had arranged with the assistance of Ensign Bernadon, U.S.N., as complete a system of defense as possible. By the kindness of the Japanese Minister, four Japanese soldiers had been sent to the legation. I had also asked for, and obtained, a Corean guard, upon whom I placed but little reliance. Early on the morning of the 6th the populace commenced to commit outrages upon the Japanese subjects residing in different parts of the city. The cry was "Death to the Japanese!" During the day numbers

Struggle for Control

were killed and their property destroyed. Several came to the legation for refuge, and I gave directions that all who came should be admitted. Between 3 and 4 o'clock P.M. we heard firing in the direction of the palace, and shortly thereafter the Japanese guard, one hundred and eighty in number, evacuated the palace grounds and marched to their legation. Along their line of march they were attacked by the people with stones and occasional shots. After they reached their legation great numbers of angry people gathered in the vicinity making threats, and occasional shots were fired. Between 4 and 5 o'clock P.M. on the 7th the Japanese soldiers and civilians left their legation grounds and marched out of the city on their way to Chemulpo. Two cannon shots were fired at them as they passed, and an occasional volley of musketry, which they returned.

The wildest excitement now prevailed. As night came on we noticed that the Japanese legation buildings were in flames. These buildings were the finest in Corea, and had just been completed, partly in the European style.

At this time there were congregated in this legation, of American citizens, myself and wife, C. L. Scudder, private secretary; Ensign J. B. Bernadon, U.S.N.; Dr. and Mrs. Allen and child, Mr. W. D. Townsend; of British subjects, W. G. Aston, esq. Her Britannic Majesty's consul-general; Mrs. Aston, Mr. E. S. B. Allen, consul's assistant; Mr. Hallifax, wife and child. Of Japanese subjects there were twenty-two men, women, and children. Fifteen Chinese and Corean servants, and a guard of twenty Corean soldiers, upon whom I placed no reliance, and only retained in the legation fearing that they might inform the populace that we were protecting Japanese.

The night was one of great anxiety, but the day dawned, and from that moment the excitement seemed to decrease. During the 6th and 7th a number of public and private buildings were burned. On the morning of the 8th I was asked to have an audience with His Majesty, who had temporarily taken up his residence at the Chinese camp. In company with the other representatives, I waited upon His Majesty. At this audience we were asked if we could consistently go to Chemulpo and have an interview with the Japanese Minister, conveying to him the earnest desire of His Majesty to maintain friendly relations with Japan. After consultation we decided to accede to His Majesty's wishes.

After the audience I took occasion to say that I had at the United States legation, and under my protection, a number of Japanese men, women, and children, and that I had determined to send them to Chemulpo under the escort of Ensign J. B. Bernadon, U.S.N., and to ask that a joint Corean and

Chinese guard be furnished for their protection. This request was seconded by the other representatives, and was acceded to by both the Corean and Chinese authorities. On the morning of the 9th Ensign Bernadon left the legation with the Japanese refugees, escorted by Corean and Chinese soldiers, and arriving safely at Chemulpo on the morning of the 10th delivered them, as directed by me, to his excellency the Japanese minister. During the night of the 10th messengers came from the King and Queen, saying that they had heard it was the intention of the foreign ladies to retire with their husbands to Chemulpo, and urging that Mrs. Foote should remain, promising her all the protection in their power, saying that her stay would do much to quiet the excitement of the people. We replied that we were the first to come and would be the last to leave. On the morning of the 10th, with His Imperial German Majesty's commissioner, Captain Zembsch, and Her Brittanic Majesty's consul-general, Mr. Aston, accompanied by his wife, I went to Chemulpo, leaving Mrs. Foote at the legation. Arriving at Chemulpo we sought for and obtained an interview with his excellency the Japanese Minister. We informed him of the sentiment of His Majesty, and afterwards engaged in an informal discussion concerning the temper of the Corean Government, as evinced by certain dispatches which had been written to the minister by the president of the Corean foreign office. We were assured by the minister that the messages of the King should be transmitted to his Government. On the following day we had other interviews, discussing certain questions of fact which had been asserted by Corean officials and denied by the Japanese minister.

On the morning of the 12th I returned alone to Seoul, His Imperial Majesty's German commissioner and Her Brittanic Majesty's consul-general deciding to remain at Chemulpo.

On the 14th I had an audience with His Majesty and reported to him the result of our interview with Mr. Takezoye. His Majesty asked me if I would accompany an envoy whom he was about to send to Japan, invoking thereby the good offices of the United States to bring about an amicable settlement between that country and Corea. I replied to him that I should prefer, first, to consult with my Government, but that the means of communication were difficult and the emergency imminent. I would consider the matter and decide at the earliest possible moment.

Recurring to the events of the 6th instant, I would say that the conflict with the Japanese troops was brought about by an attempt of the Chinese troops to force their way into the palace grounds, ostensibly to protect the King. In this attack the Corean troops joined forces with the Chinese.

Struggle for Control

During the engagement the King determined to seek a place of greater safety. "Learning this fact," as Mr. Takezoye, the Japanese minister says in a note to me, "I took my leave of His Majesty and withdrew with the Japanese guard."

Lucius H. Foote

(enclosure in No. 128)

Report of information relative to the revolutionary attempt in Seoul, Corea, by Ensign George C. Foulk, December 4–7, 1884.

The Government of Corea has been for an indefinite period under the practical control of the Min family, of which the Queen of Corea is at present the highest representative. The blood of this family is largely Chinese, and it has been always, and remains, the desire and aim of this family to subject, and retain in subjection, their country to the suzerainity of China. Members of this family are accorded special privileges by China, and are, to the exclusion of other Corean noble families, on comparatively social terms with the court of China, which they visit frequently. The family is very large, and includes the highest number of great nobles, with the greatest landed estates, of all the families of the nobility in Corea. Political differences of the several degrees of strength have long existed between this family and that of the King and a large body of the other nobles.

The Queen is a woman of strong will and considerable ability. The great body of the Corean people at large know little or nothing of the politics of their Government, nor do they dare to use any information which they may by chance possess on Government affairs. They only know their King, for whom, so far as my own experience and observation goes, they hold unbounded reverence and affection. It is, however, ground deeply into the whole Corean nation, so far as the people are concerned, that their's is the "little house" of China. Chinese coming among them are detested for their appearance, conduct, and customs; yet nothing a Chinaman might do in the course of his association with the common people would prompt a blow from any of them, for he is a "Ta-kuk-in" a man of the "great country." Japanese, on the contrary, are even admired by the Coreans of the present day for their appearance, customs, and conduct; yet against them lies a deep current of hereditary hatred for their alleged cruelties in their ancient invasions of Corea, and the Coreans are always ready for the licsence when they may vent this feeling in shedding Japanese blood.

The first Corean nobles to leave their country to visit a progressive one, were So Kwang Pom and Kim Ok Kiun. These two men, nine years ago, left Corea secretly and visited Japan; upon their return to Corea, they went boldly before the King and described what they had seen. In later years other Corean nobles visited Japan and China; of these, however, until within the past two years, but one, Pak Yong Hyo, joined the two above named in their aim towards adopting Western civilization for Corea and advocated openly such a policy.

The family of So is claimed to be truly Corean, and is highly illustrious for the number of just and wise officers it has produced; it has no superior in Corea in regard to this and ancient, creditable ancestry.

The family of Kim is likewise regarded as truly Corean; it is remarkable for its extent and antiquity. Pak Yong Hyo is also of an ancient family, and is the brother-in-law of the King, bearing as such the title of royalty Kum-oi-nung, which by the ancient law, forbade his holding actual office in the government.

Prior to the revolt of the troops in Seoul in 1882, under the Tai Wen Kun, So and Kim, who held nightly discussions of the civilization problem, and were endeavoring to induce Min Yong Ik and several other young nobles to join them, were charged by the fanatical Tai Wen Kun with endeavoring to introduce Christianity into Corea, and both came very near losing their heads. The Tai Wen Kun was the ex-regent and the father of the King; long after his regency had ceased he held the administrative power of the Government, and directed his great energy with fanatical zeal against the efforts of the Jesuit fathers and Christian Coreans to extend Christianity in Corea.

The members of the Corean Embassy to the United States have repeatedly told me that the number of Coreans executed after torture by him for professing Christianity or being suspected of it can only be reckoned by the tens of thousands; also that his fanatical hatred of the foreign religion was mainly due to the raid upon the grave of one of his ancestors by the German Jew Oppert.

Obedient to the will and direction of China the Mins were pre-eminent among Corean nobles in conducting for Corea the negotiations for a treaty with the United States, in May, 1882, at Inchun, on which occasion Admiral Shufeldt represented the United States Government, having come there in the U.S.S. Swatara.

This energy of the Mins has given them the mistaken reputation of being members of the progress party in Corea; in fact they only acted in obedience to their hereditary lord, China, without a thought patriotic to Corea, beyond that they in common with all Coreans at that time felt the danger of a seizure of a part of Corea by Russia. By the King of Corea and the true progress party of three the treaty with the United States was hailed as the forerunner of complete independence from China.

To the call of China for Corea to treat with the United States for their several reasons, all the chief members of the Corean Government were obedient, but the Tai-Wen-Kun, who though purely patriotic to Corea, only saw in making treaties with western powers the means of introducing broadcast hated Christianity. It is natural therefore that he should be at enmity with the Mins who were negotiating the treaty with Admiral Shufeldt.

Consequently, in July 1882, we find that, taking advantage of disaffection among soldiers of the capital, occasioned by short rations, issued by the Mins, he

Struggle for Control

directs their revolt against that family, and having disposed of its members, seizes the Government itself.

Many Mins were killed; Min Thai Ho (father of Min Yong Ik) was left supposed to be fatally wounded in a ditch; poison was to be administered to the Queen, but a maid personating her in disguise, took the poison and died while the Queen escaped. Min Yong Ik shaved his head and after hiding in the mountains three days, walked to Fusan whence he escaped to Japan in the disguise of a Buddist priest. For his disobedience to its command and his attempt to annihilate its loyal servants, the Mins, the Chinese Government sent its troops to Corea and carried off in banishment the Tai-wen-Kun; the power of the Mins for China having been greatly cut off by the revolt. Chinese troops were placed in Seoul to strengthen the remainder and have remained there ever since. It has been said that the Chinese did not execute the Tai-wen-Kun, because he was the father of the King; this is true if it be explained that such an action as executing the father of the King would have embittered the masses of the common people against the Mins and China, and probably to the extent of open rebellion against China. At the time of the revolt under the Tai-wen-Kun there were no Chinese in Corea, nor had there been for more than a hundred years. In Seoul, however, resided a Japanese minister with a small guard of Japanese soldiers.

The news of the revolt of the soldiers under the Tai-wen-Kun went to Japan first, and at once that Government prepared a force to send to the assistance of the Japanese minister in Seoul. The Chinese consul at Nagasaki telegraphed to China that the Japanese were sending a force to seize Corea; this at least was the substance of what was told three Corean nobles, then at Tientsin in China, by the Chinese authorities there. These Corean nobles were, in order of rank, Cho Yong Ha, Kim Yun Sik, and O-Yun Chung.

Cho was a noted Chinese scholar and a strong Confucianist. Min Yong Ik has represented to me that Cho and his companions at Tien-Tsin held powers plenipotentiary; this, however, is emphatically denied by So Kwang Pom and the progressive party, who say that such powers were simply assumed, such deliberate assumption of the King's powers being no unusual thing for members of the Min faction. Knowing that Corea was helpless after the revolt of the soldiers to resist an invasion of the Japanese, Cho applied to the deputy viceroy at Tien-Tsin (Li Hung Chang then being absent, in mourning for his mother) for the use of Chinese troops which he might take to Corea. His first appeal was refused, but on the second, made by him as holding powers plenipotentiary, the use of the soldiers was granted him; Cho and his companions came to Chemulpo with the soldiers on board Chinese vessels of war.

At the time the news of the revolt came to Japan there were two Corean nobles residing in Tokio; these were Kim Ok Kiun and So Kwang Pom, who had gone there with an ambassador and remained behind to study and make purchases. They heard that the Japanese were about to send an expedition to Corea, and the rumor that it was to seize their country.

Going at once to the minister for foreign affairs in Japan, they made inquiry as to the exact object of the expedition, and were assured that Japan had no intention to seize Corea, and only sent a force there to protect her subjects in Corea. Satisfied with this Kim and So proceeded to Corea at once arriving at Chemulpo with the Japanese force. They had realized that the Tai-wen-Kun's revolt endangered their hopes of independence and progress for Corea by giving the Chinese a new lien upon them; and anticipating that Cho would bring Chinese soldiers to Chemulpo, had drawn up during the voyage from Japan a series of arguments in writing against the employment by Corea of Chinese troops in Seoul, and favoring the use of Japanese force to restore order there.

The Japanese force with So and Kim, and the Chinese force with Cho and his companions, arrived at Chemulpo at about the same time, and while neither force was yet landed, the two parties of Corean officers discovered each other. A consultation ensued between them, in which So and Kim used every argument in their power to induce Cho to abandon the use of Chinese troops. They argued more particularly that as Japan had a legation in Seoul to protect, she had every right to send troops there; the use of the Chinese, however, could be called for on no ground except such as would give China the opportunity of tightening more firmly than ever the grip on Corea she had loosened in aiding and permitting the American treaty negotiations three months before.

After a prolonged discussion, which grew hot towards the end, it was agreed to by all that, if practicable, to the King should be submitted the question, "Should the Chinese land and enter Seoul or not?" Kim Ok Kiun, disguised as a low Corean, then went to Seoul to submit the question to the King. He found the Tai-wen-Kun (his bitter enemy) in charge of the King's person, his friends driven away, and that it would be impossible to reach the King. His mission having failed, he returned to Chemulpo, soon after which the Chinese force landed and entered the capitol. The Tai-wen-Kun was abducted, order restored, and affairs settled into the condition found in Corea on the arrival of Minister Foote.

The Chinese force took up permanent quarters in extensive camps within the walls; almost by the palace gate they erected a fort, as well as two others outside of the city near the approaches from the river Han—these two for use in case of invasion against the advance of a Japanese army towards Seoul. The number of troops landed was augmented a little later to 3,000 men, which number remianed in Seoul until June of 1884 when it was reduced to 1,500. A Chinese commissioner arrived in October, 1883.

It has been positively stated to me, though not until they seemed forced to divulge it, by So Kwang Pom and Kim Ok Kiun, that the result of this use of Chinese troops was the enactment of a new agreement between China and Corea, by which the Chinese obtained such rights in Corea as made her more intimately a dependency of China than had ever been the case before. The full particulars of this agreement had not been (on principle) divulged to the western

Struggle for Control

world by either Corea or China; nor could either have well done so. It was undoubtedly the effect of this new agreement with China, originated by Cho-Yong Ha, and the execution of its terms willingly abetted and enforced by the Mins, which drove the progressive and truly loyal party in Corea to the extreme measure taken by them in the revolutionary attempt of December 4-7 last.

The King and the progressive Coreans looked upon the American treaty as the wedge which, at least politically, freed Corea from China, and it was hailed by them with great joy. It may then be understood how great was their chagrin to find Corea, by the action of Cho and the Mins before the American treaty was yet ratified, placed anew and more rigidly than ever subservient to China. Thinking that the new status of Corea to China would be understood abroad, they feared that the American treaty would never be ratified, consequently, I have been told repeatedly, "His Majesty danced for joy when Minister Foote arrived."

This meant to them one of two things, namely: That the United States understood the real relations between China and Corea and meant at all hazards to claim independence for Corea; or that the United States did not know of the real status of Corea, in which case, by concealment of the late agreement with China, Corea still had a hope of becoming free, through the effect of her being regarded as independent in the relations between her and the United States. The mission to the United States Government, headed by Min Yong Ik, in 1884, determined for the King and the progressive men (represented in the embassy by So Kwang Pom alone) that the latter view was correct, and they regulated their line of action accordingly.

At the time the Corean embassy was in the United States, Kim Ok Kiun—(the oldest of the progressive party of three and its leader in all active measures) was in Japan and in regular correspondence with So Kwang Pom with the embassy. These two men of all Corea were the only ones who possessed any knowledge of the principles of western government; they had both made long visits to Japan, were naturally highly intelligent, and had entered with great perseverence and energy into the progressive spirit of the official classes of Japan; both had been in effect pupils of Fukuzawa, the distinguished leader of Japan in political progress. Both, but particularly So Kwang Pom, were noted among foreigners of all classes who had met them as frank, intelligent, active, useful men. In Corea they and their families were respected and beloved for their just conduct as officials.

With a view to organizing an efficient military force for Corea to replace that loaned by China, the Corean Government had after the revolt of 1882 established four batallions of Corean soldiers, and to furnish officers for these, through Kim and So, fourteen Corean young men, many of whom were sent to Japan to pursue a course of study and exercise in the Government military school in Tokio. The leader of these students was So Che Pil, a near relative of So Kwang Pom. During their preparation, the troops were placed under the instruction of Chinese officers, procured for this service by the Mins and Cho-Yong Ha. Kim was much in Japan overseeing the instruction of the students, as well as directing the efforts of other Coreans who had been gotten there, largely through his energy, to study manufactures and trade, and to make purchases of certain machinery and furniture, upholstery, &c., the latter for the palace. Kim's rank of nobility corresponds to that of baron, and his office is president of the department for the improvement and colonization of waste lands. As this embodied intercourse with foreign countries, he was later made a vice-president of the foreign office.

Pak Yong-Hyo, by ancient Corean law could not hold office, yet the King assigned to him the office of mayor of Seoul. He was not familiar with any foreign language and was much less advanced in progressive ideas than So and Kim; he was, however, earnestly and rather hot-headedly progressive, and entered into reform in Seoul with such over-energy that loud complaints came from the common people, encouraged by the conservative faction, which soon resulted in his removal from office. The anger of the Mins was particularly aroused at the departure from the ancient law as shown in his being given an office by the King.

All the above evidences of progress in Corea are embraced in the interval between the revolt in 1882 and the return of the embassy from the United States in May, 1884. All the work of the three progressive leaders was warmly aided by the King, who had ample opportunities of time at least for encouraging it, the actual machinery of his internal government being worked entirely by the Mins, and in which he had little or no power to act.

A part of the embassy to the United States, headed by the vice minister, Hong Yong Sik, returned to Corea in the winter of 1883. From this time dates Hong's connection with the progressive party. He expressed himself as having been in a—"light so bright as to dazzle him." He entered into the progressive spirit of the King's party with great caution, however, as was always regarded by So and Kim as too slow or aggravatingly indecisive. He received the appointment of postmaster-general from the King, but for a long interval little was done by him toward establishing a postal system. With Hong, Cheu Kyung Sok returned from America, bringing with him the generous supply of seeds furnished by the Department of Agriculture.

He was promptly granted a large tract of valuable land, which he very commendably converted into what is now known as the American farm.

In May the Trenton arrived at Chemulpo, having on board Min Yong Ik, So Kwong Pom, and Pyon Su, with whom I had lived in the closest possible friendship during eight months. Min Yong Ik, the chief of the embassy, had seemed sincere in expressions of his intention to use his utmost energy toward the development of his country, yet I had long since observed that he was faint hearted and very changeable in disposition; and his constant study of Confucian books he carried on I deemed sadly at the expense of what should have been to him invaluable opportunities for observation and enlightenment. So Kwang Pom and Pyon Su were, however, indefatigable in compiling notes on useful subjects, and

Struggle for Control

from encyclopedia sources, through my translations, they brought home a great mass of information on the political and progressive histories of the principle countries of the world.

On June 2, in a gay procession I went to Seoul with these members of the embassy. On the way, So Kwang Pom took occasion to say to me that he greatly feared that the ambassador, Min Yong Ik, in spite of all that had been done for him, and however good his intentions had been while abroad, might be turned directly to the opposite of what might be expected from him; that what he had learned and seen through his Confucian training and the hereditary instincts of his family, might be employed, after the manner of the Chinese, against Western progress.

The reception of the ambassador in Seoul was enthusiastic. All parties seemed to join in it. The visit of the officers of the Trenton, the expression of good feeling exchanged between the Corean and American Governments and of their officers, these with much else seemed to strengthen the progressive influence in Seoul.

A shadow fell, however, on the King and the progressive men when they learned that Admiral Shufeldt was not soon to arrive in Korea, for the embassy had brought word that he was to arrive in Corea in May. It was then supposed that military officers from the United States would probably arrive with Admiral Shufeldt.

Soon after his arrival Min Yong Ik became a vice-president of the foreign office; So Kwang Pom was elevated in the order of nobility, and Pyon Su, heretofore not an officer in the Government, was made a chusa, by virtue of which rank he was given direct access to the King. The progressive party, now strengthened by the addition of these members of the embassy to the United States, was in high hopes, and with the King himself as their director, began a series of preparations for a vigorous infusion of Western civilization into Corea. Evidently, however, all great measures were not to be taken in this direction until the Chinese troops had left Seoul, in effecting which the services of an adviser, and indirectly those of other persons soon expected from the United States, were believed to be efficient. It was not long before the Chinese instructors of the Corean troops were dismissed by the King, a charge of cruel treatment having been brought against them. This was followed by the acceptance of the resignation of Mr. P. G. Von Mollendorff from the foreign office, in which he had had great influence as adviser. The creation of these vacancies was too significant to make commentary necessary. Arms were also purchased, and under my direction, as requested, stored away carefully in the palace grounds. From Japan, to execute contracts made by Kim Ok Kiun, came a number of qualified Japanese, who were held in readiness to begin teaching the use of machinery, the manufacture of paper, pottery &c.

Steps were also taken toward securing a director of agriculture, school teachers, and several other foreigners for service under the Corean Government.

In regard to these, the initiatory steps were taken in consultations of the progressive leaders, including the King, in which I was warmly invited to have a voice. I was also daily visited by Pyon Chusa, who came direct from the King with requests for services of different kinds. These I obeyed whenever permitted by my instructions. Upon the occasion of being asked by His Majesty to order for him an electric light plant for the palace, I declined, until it was explained to me that it was also meant to extend the right to furnish electrical apparatus to the United States; that such rights had just been refused to the British consul-general, and that courtesy would prevent the immediate granting of such rights to the United States minister, who it was known held an application to do so from Mr. Thomas A. Edison. The electric-light plant I only ordered when assured that $10,000 had been secured to make prompt payment. I also ordered and paid for six head of breeding stock, purchased in California, for the Corea-American farm, to which His Majesty had added an extension of some 8 miles square for breeding purposes.

In July the fourteen Corean military students returned from Japan, and were enthusiastically greeted by the progressive men. They were exercised before the King and gave great satisfaction. A few were given appointments in the batallion of the palace guard commanded by General Han Kin Chik at once.

Min Yong Ik soon showed the effects of the influence brought to bear upon him by his family. First he endeavored to pay a visit to China, which the progressive men regarded with dissatisfaction, believing it to be intended as a make-peace visit to offset any ill-impressions in the Chinese court due to his long association with Western foreigners. This he deferred, however, and originated the idea of changing the national dress in certain details, most prominent of which were the tightening of belts and narrowing the sleeves. This, too, was unsatisfactory to the progressive party, who saw in the change an approach to the Chinese costume, or food for an excuse against the move they contemplated, which was permitting freedom in matters of dress. Min Yong Ik's scheme became a law, and by royal edict the changes in costume were effected by a fixed date.

Suddenly Min Yonk Ik resigned from the foreign office and received an appointment as general in command of the Right Palace Guard Battalion. This was immediately following a discussion before His Majesty between himself and So Kwang Pom, in which the King decided a question in favor of the latter. Word had been received through me that Admiral Shufeldt, then expected by every steamer, had not yet left America, and that he would only come to Corea at once upon a formal invitation to do so by the King. This delay in his coming, as well as that of the military officers, left the Government in an embarrassed position, as it was without any adviser in the foreign office of instruction officers in the new army.

Min Yong Ik then proposed, as suggested by the Chinese commissioner, Chen Shu Yang, that ex-Consul-General Denny be at once invited to accept the

Struggle for Control

position of adviser in place of Admiral Shufeldt. So Kwang Pom opposed this, and it was in a discussion of this question in which the King with much firmness favored So Kwang Pom. A telegraphic message was sent at once through General Foote to Admiral Shufeldt to "come at once."

A little later, and through Min-Yong-Ik, five Chinese instructors were called from China for service with the Corean army. This created a great sensation among the progressive men, but it was most disasterous to the fourteen students who, by the employment of the Chinese instructors, were thrown clear of any chance of holding military offices consistent with their rank as Corean citizens, to say the least. With the exception of three employed in General Han's batallion, the students were turned entirely adrift from military service and given subordinate positions, out of half charity, by the progressive leaders, in the post office department, under Hong Yong Sik.

By September of 1884, Min-Yong-Ik was entirely clear of the progressive party. His associates were Chinese, and the strongest members of the Pro-Chinese faction; he did not receive visits from Western foreigners in the daytime, and on several occasions showed contemptuous insolence in their presence. In August a Corean officer of high grade was openly seized by a party of Chinese soldiers and beaten so severely by them in the street that his life was despaired of; this was the outcome of a quarrel between the Chinese commissioner and the Corean officer about the right of passage through a gateway of the Corean officer's house, which was next to that of the Chinese officer.

After having been beaten, the Corean officer was held as a prisoner in a Chinese house until released by the interference of the British consul-general, Mr. Aston. Min-Yong-Ik's indifference to an appeal to him for action against the Chinese in this case served only to strengthen the feeling against him of the progressive men, and of the common people against his family.

During the autumn the numbers of Chinese in Seoul increased rapidly, and the foreign office business was reported to be almost entirely confined to actions of Chinese against Coreans for debt. Chinese began to extend their homes and trading places into the country; they came and went as they pleased without passports. Mr. P. G. Von Möllendorf had again practically become the adviser in the foreign office.

In September and October some of the Japanese who had long been waiting for employment under the contracts arranged by Kim-Ok-Kiun began to push their claims through their legation.

The new army at this time consisted of the four palace guard battalions, in aggregate 5,500 men, of whom 3,000 were armed with Peabody-Martini rifles. The battalions were commanded by Generals Min-Yong-Ik, Cho-Yong-Ha, and I-jo-yun of the strong Chinese faction, and General Han-Kin-Chik; the latter officer had at first been regarded as one of the progressive party, but latterly I was told that his real political status was doubtful; that at heart he was progressive, but feared the opposition of the Chinese party. However his real status may have been, it was in his battalion only that the military students were employed, and he was on friendly terms with the progressive men.

This officer, Han-Kin-Chik, was the highest general in rank, and as such he was the representative head of the Government in the great guild among the common people, called pusang, which may be likened to a great body of militia. It was by the invitation of this officer that I was conducted through the Pukhan Mountain fortress in Seoul, with the view of obtaining advice from me as to sites for certain new forts. Reference is made to this in a report on my first journey into the interior of Corea.

The attitude of the Japanese in Seoul had always been such as to indicate an earnest desire to aid the progress party and to be on peaceable friendly terms with the people. The conduct of Japanese citizens toward Coreans was commendable. Indicating great consideration on the part of the Japanese Government towards Corea, was the restraint placed upon Japanese merchants establishing themselves in Seoul by the Japanese minister, who evidently in doing so followed the spirit of the treaties by which the capital was not to be thrown open to trade if the Chinese left.

In October one of the progressive party leaders told me that unless foreign intervention prevented, Corea would soon be irreclaimably in the hands of the Chinese, and with great bitterness went on to say that his small party had not only lost power to proceed further and had been receding, but they were in actual danger of execution; that this might follow any charge made against them by the Chinese faction. He also stated that part of the King's revenue meant to be used by the King through them to fulfill all progressive contracts had been cut off from him by the Mins, (notably through Min-Thai-Ho, who controlled the chief revenues), and was being used to pay Chinese instructors and equip Corean soldiers with a view to amalgamation with the Chinese army.

Having heard on unquestionable authority that certain Chinese officers had informed some Corean officers of the Chinese faction that in case of war French ships would be fired on by Chinese from Corean territory, I believe that the Mins have been preparing in obedience to the will of China, their contingent of Corean troops for the use of China in the war with France. In December the annual tribute of Corea to China was to start overland for Peking in charge of the usual procession of ambassadors and underlings, numbering in all about one hundred persons; it is more than likely that, with the tribute party in this December, it was intended that Corean troops should go to Peking; above all things this would move the progressive party to desperate action.

On October 25 one of the progressive leaders called upon me, and at once began to speak passionately of the unfortunate situation of the King and his party. Later, with deliberation, he stated that for the sake of Corea, Min-Thai-Ho, Cho-Yong-Ha, the four generals and four other lower officials possibly, would have to be killed. Though the officer was passionate in his manner, he was one whom I had always found positive and correct in his statements to me; his words, therefore, did not seem empty to me, and I became indignant that he should communicate such an idea to me. A few sharp words passed between us and he then quieted down.

On October 26, during a call on Min Yong Ik, I learned that the separation of the two parties was so wide as to prevent any discussion of public affairs in which officers of the two parties might be brought together; this convinced me that a crisis was near at hand and one which would probably result in bloodshedding and violence not confined to the official classes of Coreans.

Prior to this I had constantly been in the habit of communicating any and all news of political interest to the United States minister, to whom I had felt this a particular duty and one which I believe would give him satisfaction, for living in the midst of the city and having intimate associates among all classes of officials, I believe I had exceptional means for obtaining useful information.

On October 28 I told him every detail of what I had heard, and expressed firmly the opinion that these were sufficient to forewarn some serious outbreak in Seoul. On October 31 I called upon Ensign Bernadon and Mr. W. D. Townsend, the two other Americans in Seoul, and told them what I believed to be the situation. On this day Hong-Yong-Sik called upon me, and I received notes from two other members of the progressive party requesting interviews; these I was forced to refuse, and on the following day I set out from Seoul to make a second journey into the interior of Corea in accordance with my instructions from the Navy Department. A report summarizing my experiences during this journey, including the period of the revolutionary attempt in Seoul I have already submitted to the Department.

I append to this a list of the officers of the Corean Government, including members of both parties, who were foremost pre-eminently in Corean politics and active duty under it, together with other notes which, in my opinion, may assist in throwing light upon the situation in Corea.

Very respectfully submitted. George C. Foulk

List of Corean Officers, with Titles, Offices, etc.

November 1884

The Pro Chinese, or Min Party

Min-T'hai-Ho—Rank, earl (poguk); a blood relative of the Queen; father of princess royal by affinity, a brother of Queen by adoption. Head of home department; treasurer for all general revenues expended for maintainence of troops of capital guard; subsistence of relatives of King's family and their dependencies, which include a large part of the population of Seoul. Father of Min-Yong-Ik. Held several other offices.

Min-Yong-Mok—Rank, count (pansoh); blood relative of the Queen; Ex-president of the foreign office. Head of military post at Poupyong and chief recruiting officer general. Held two other offices.

Min-Ung-Sik—Rank, count (pansoh); blood relative of Queen. Recently given in addition to other offices, office of kaussa, governor of Pyongan province (Chinese border), and was engaged in equipping provincial troops.

Min-Yong-Ik—Rank, prince; by affinity, through adoption, nephew to Queen, to whom is nearest relative through the Min (deceased) who adopted him from his natural father Min-T'hai-Ho; this made him court favorite as also champau (assistant) in board of ceremonies; but his chief office is general of right palace guard battalion.

Cho-Yong-Ha—Rank, earl (poguk); by marriage related to Mins. Greatly beloved by people for justice and generosity; bore honorable title "loyal knight" for meritorious service to the King. Since 1882 not in favor in King's court; out of active office, yet active in all business between China and Corea, a fluent Chinese scholar; arranged contract for employment of Von Mollendorf.

I-jo-Yun—Rank, marquis (champau); a strong member of the faction; commanded left guard battalion of palace.

Yun-Tae-Jun—Rank, marquis (champau); a rank Confucianist. Champau (assistant) in board of justice; ex-vice president of foreign office; commanded rear battalion of palace guard.

Kim-Hong-Chip—Rank, count; president of foreign office; had risen rapidly; noted for obstinate hatred of Christianity and having torn up a copy of Scriptures presented to board of which he was a member to decide as to whether it was a fit volumne for the King to have.

Kim-yun-Sik—Rank, marquis (champau), vice president of foreign office; one of nobles who brought Chinese troops to Seoul in 1882.

Shim-S'hang-Un—Rank, marquis (champau), governor of capital province.

O-Yun-Chung—Rank, marquis (champau) vice head of one of the six boards; one of the nobles who brought Chinese troops to Seoul in 1882.

Kim-Kin-Pok—Chief eunuch, head of palace household department and in constant attendance upon the Queen.

The above officers were leaders; each held large estates, and resided in extensive establishments in Seoul, connected with each of which was a great body of underlings of various grades. Besides there are many other high nobles as well as others of lower grades, but not active in international affairs of the Government.

The Progress Party

Hong-Yong-Sik—Rank, count (pansoh) postmaster general; of an illustrious Corean family; vice-minister in embassy to United States. Held office in one of the six boards.

Struggle for Control

Kim-Ok-Kiun—Rank, marquis (champau), vice-president foreign office, head of colonization department; chief of progress party; extremeist.

So-Kwang-Pom—Rank, baron (chamise); held also special rank of nobility called takiyo, by virtue of which was near person of the King constantly; held office in home department; secretary to embassy of the United States, as regarded abroad; was third minister in embassy and sent with it specially for the King's service.

Pak-Yong-Hyo—Rank, prince (kum-oi-nung); brother-in-law to King; not in office; had been mayor of Seoul: in title, first in rank of progress party; extremeist.

Han-Kin-Chik—Rank, count (pansoh); relative of So Kwang Pom; general commanding front palace guard battalion; government head of the guild called pausang, a large body resembling militia among lower orders of people; long a doubtful member of the progress party.

Pyon-Su—Rank, chusa (no English equivalent); member of embassy to the United States; actively engaged in progressive affairs for the King; had long resided in Japan.

Other than the above-named progressive officers there were a few officers of low rank who were inactive members; a small body of the middle class among the people favored them.

Mok-Champau is the Corean title of Mr. P. G. Von Mollendorf, who regards himself as a Corean subject; rank, marquis, vice-president of foreign office; had at one time held four different offices; head of Corean customs; practically, foreign adviser of the Government; an active member of the pro-Chinese party, and highly influential, mainly through Cho-Yong-Ha, Kim-Hong-Chip and Min-Yong-Mok.

NO. 131   Dec. 19 / 84.

Secretary of State

Sir:

On the 5th inst. I wrote a communication to Rear Admiral Jno. Lee Davis, commanding U. S. Naval Forces in this Station informing him of the attempted assassination of Min Yong Ik and of the events immediately following. He received my dispatch on the 13th inst. at Nagasaki, and left on the same afternoon with the Flag Ship "Trenton." for Chemulpo, arriving on the 17th inst. He at once placed himself in communication with me at Söul and on the 18th inst. sent to me a guard of ten marines in charge of Lieut. K [?] and Ensign Haessler of his staff, with orders to report to me for such duty as I might assign to him. It is now my intention to go to Chemulpo on the 22d inst. leaving Lieut Foulke temporarily in charge with instructions that if any sudden outbreak occurs to leave the Legation property in charge of the Corean Government and return at once to Chemulpo. I anticipate no exigency of this kind, unless war should be inaugurated between Corea and Japan or between Japan and China, in which event the Corean Government would be entirely powerless to protect us against the lawlessness of its own people. I go to Chemulpo because all the Diplomatic and Consulor Officials, save the Chinese Commissioner are there, and that I may be at hand in case there is any inclination to bring about an amicable understanding, perhaps by the good offices of the Foreign Representatives.

Lucius H. Foote

NO. 135. Dec. 29 / 84

Secretary of State

Sir:

His Excellency Kim Hong Chip Prime Minister, as also the President of the Foreign Office have had interviews with me in reference to the situation. I have advised prudence and conciliation and am of the opinion that if the Japanese Government is willing to listen to terms and is not too exorbitant in its demands, an amicable arrangement can be brought about. Great consternation exists, and many of the inhabitants are leaving the city. Otherwise everything is quiet. It is rumored that a Chinese Ambassador of high rank, with a force of Chinese troops has already arrived at Masampo, a Station on the Corean Coast.

Lucius H. Foote

NO. 136. December 31, 1884.

Secretary of State

Sir:

I have just received a note from Count Inouye Kaoru, H.I.J.M' Secretary of State, informing me that he has arrived at Chemulpo as Special Am-

Struggle for Control

bassador "for the purpose of settling the difficulty which has recently arisen," and expressing a desire to see me if possible before his arrival at the Capital. As he leaves for Seoul tomorrow, I shall await his arrival here.

Lucius H. Foote

NO. 137.　　　　　　　　　　　　　　　　　　　　　　　　Jany 1, 1885.

Secretary of State

Sir:

An Imperial Ambassador with a force of troops estimated at three thousand, arrived in Seoul to day. I learn also that twenty five hundred men have arrived with H.I.J.M' Ambassador. It is to be hoped that no irritation may result from this fresh arrival of Soldiers. The settlement of the difficulties will depend very much upon the temper manifested by the Representatives of the two Governments. It would hardly seem possible that China would be willing at this time, to take on new complications. For this reason I hope for an amicable adjustment.

Lucius H. Foote

NO. 138.　　　　　　　　*Confidential*　　　　　　　　January 2, 1885.

Secretary of State

Sir:

I have just returned from an interview with H.I.J.M' Ambassador Count Inouye, in which the situation was discussed and my opinion asked upon many points. As far as it seemed prudent I had no hesitation in talking freely with him. I said to him, that any adjustment which involved the disintegration of any portion of Corean Territory would, in my opinion, be most unwise. I found to my satisfaction that he fully agreed with me upon this point. I urged upon him that Japan could afford to treat Corea liberally and at the same time maintain her own honor. He said that his Government desired an amicable adjustment, that questions between Japan and Corea, and those between Japan and China must be treated separately that he should exact first, from the Corean Gov't, an apology, and, secondly, a money indemnity, that the amount of the indemnity would not exceed one hundred and fifty Thousand dollars. I came from the interview with the full conviction that, as far as Japan is concerned, there would be a wise, prudent and liberal policy pursued.

Lucius H. Foote

NO. 139.   Jany 4, 1885

Secretary of State

Sir:

Kim Hong Chip, Corean Prime Minister has been appointed Plenipotentiary with full powers to negotiate with the Japanese Ambassador. I can see nothing now, in the way of a speedy adjustment of the difficulties. The Chinese Ambassador informs me that he is instructed to use his utmost endeavors to bring about an amicable settlement, he says frankly however, that he has no powers to settle questions which may have arisen between China and Japan.

Lucius H. Foote

NO. 146.   January 31, 1885.

Secretary of State

Sir:

I have the honor to submit the following relative to the situation in Korea.

His Majesty, the King is authoritatively stated to have yielded the administration of the government exclusively, to the Oi Jöng Pu, or Ministerial body upon the demand of the conservative faction of the government. This faction has also demanded the execution of Kim Ok Kiun and four others of the late conspiracy, all of whom are now in Japan, to which they scaped immediately after the late revolutionary attempt.

His Majesty, exhausted with care and business consequent upon the recent difficulties and augmented by exposure has been quite ill, but is now recovering.

The torture and trials of twelve persons implicated in the conspiracy were concluded on the 27th instant, and they were sentenced to death; six were executed a few hundred yards from this Legation, and five on the main street of the city on the 28th and 29th instants respectively. These persons were placed face down in the streets and decapitated by from six to ten blows of a dull instrument, while a rope secured to their queues served to open the wounds. The bodies were all dismembered and distributed about the streets for exposure for three or four days. The twelfth victim died in prison from voluntary starvation and the effects of his torture. Of these twelve persons, one was a student of high birth; the others were underlings and headmen of the houses of the conspirators.

A great number of other persons have been hunted down and tortured; this augmented the consternation which already existed after the revolt, and thousands of citizens fled from the city; these are now returning and the populace in general is quieting down.

The two Chinese Embassadors yet remain in the city with a considerable body of troops. The Japanese Legation, temporarily outside the West Gate of the city, is in charge of a Chargé d'Affaire, and is the headquarters of 600 Japanese soldiers under the command of a Colonel. Japanese civilians come into the city, but through distrust on the part of the Koreans, may not rent quarters within the walls. The other Powers (except Russia and Italy which have no representatives in Korea), namely, England and Germany, are represented by an Acting Consul General and an Acting Commissioner respectively.

I have reason to believe that active foreign intercourse of the Korean Foreign Office is as yet confined to this Legation; this I inaugurated as soon as the Foreign Office had recovered sufficiently from the paralyzing effects of the emeute in attempting to ascertain the position of the Government and His Majesty with regard to contracts made with Americans before the attempted revolt. These were exclusively originated in the King's name, I find, and by his authority; while the way is not entirely clear as to their fulfillment, the outlook to this effect is favorable, precluding, of course, any new difficulties.

George C. Foulk

NO. 177.   May 30, 1885.

Secretary of State

Sir:

I have the honor to report that affairs in Korea are in a more peaceful and harmonious state than at any time heretofore since the disturbances of December last. Serious apprehension, which had been giving rise to disturbing rumors, was allayed by the happy termination of the Conference at Peking between Japan and China.

At present, the chief topic of speculation among the Korean officers and the nobles is the expected return of the Tai-wen-Kun, the father of the King and ex-regent, who was carried to China after the revolt of the troops of Seoul in 1882: his return is expected as one of the results of the Peking conference. By a large class of the most powerful nobles, who are influential through connection with the family of the Queen, the return of the Tai-wen-Kun is greatly dreaded, as his having been carried to China was due to his attempt to cut off their influence in 1882, and even to remove the Queen. An Embassy of three members was appointed by His Majesty to go to China to bring back the Tai-wen-Kun early in this month, but it has not yet started, the delay being stated to be due to the opposition of the Queen's party to the return of the Tai-wen-Kun.

By the masses of the people the possible return of the Tai-wen-Kun would seem to be hailed with pleasure. He is known to be a man of much firmness of character, of great ability and great power among the people, and more particularly as being an intensely patriotic Korean. While foreigners in Korea are unable to foretell the effects of his return, the generally express satisfaction at its possibility under the hope that he may introduce the spirit of firmness and decision now so lamentably absent in the Government. The Tai-wen-Kun is now about sixty-seven years old, but yet physically and mentally sound and energetic.

In March last, the people of the district, called Yōjū rose in arms against the local governor, or Pusa, in an attempt to resist excessive and illegal taxation: they destroyed the governor's house and seriously injured a number of his agents. The governor was a member of the Min family of nobles, against which feeling is strong all over the country. Troops were promptly sent to Yōjū, the rebellion quelled, and the governor removed and punished.

During the present month a similar rebellion broke out at the capital (Wonjū) of Kangwon province, directed here also against the governor who was also a Min. A stockade was built about the yamun, three of the

Struggle for Control

agents burnt to death and the governor injured and forced to flee for his life. The effects of these events has been to create great alarm in the great family of Mins, and the report that there was a general movement among the people to exterminate the whole family. Min Yong Ik, who was the Embassador to the United States is still in the country, acting as Ōsa, or detective officer upon the local governments; he is accompanied by a guard of forty soldiers: his real object in living thus is fear for his life.

Feeling against the conspirators who fled to Japan has weakened very greatly, notwithstanding the bitter vigilance of the present government to check any movement or speech in their favor. The friends and families of these men remain are unharmed and free. No other punishments than those already reported (i.e.–the execution of eleven persons and death of one from torture) have been made the Government of persons implicated in the conspiracy of December.

The Government is slowly and with difficulty paying its indemnity to Japan; the first payment of twenty-five thousand dollars was made during the present month.

A military court is now trying a Japanese soldier who bayonetted and killed a Chinese servant in the Japanese lines, in March last.

George C. Foulk

NO. 199. July 10, 1885.

Secretary of State

Sir:

I have the honor to report that orders have been received here by the Chinese authorities in Seoul from their government to effect the complete withdrawal of the Chinese troops now in Seoul on the 22d instant. They will embark at Masampho in vessels of the firm of Russel & Co of Shanghai.

The Japanese Government removed its soldiers a week since, leaving but a guard of 80 for the legation.

It is now understood that an embassy will at once go to China to bring back the Tai-wen Kun, the father of the King, and ex-Regent, who has been retained in China since 1882.

Unquestionably the return of the Tai-wen Kun is eagerly hoped for by the people of Korea, and equally dreaded by a large class of nobles, chief of whom are the Queen's or great Min family. As to the future influence of the Tai-wen Kun, or his policy of action after his long absence in China, nothing can be definitely known.

As the withdrawal of the Chinese and Japanese troops includes that of the Chinese instructors who have served with the Korean soldiers of the capital, the latter are to be left without any assuredly competent directing officers; under the circumstances, the foreign representatives unanimously regard the departure of the Chinese and Japanese with some feelings of apprehension and regret.

George C. Foulk

NO. 211 August 4, 1885.

Secretary of State

Sir,

I have to report that on the 27th ultimo, His Majesty, the King of Korea dismissed Mr. P. G. Von Möllendorff from the Foreign Office, in which he has been acting as Vice President and Adviser holding the title and rank of a Korean noble. His dismissal from the Custom's service will follow as soon as the Government shall have ascertained its positions with regard to a great number of contracts and schemes into which it has been drawn by Mr. Von Möllendorff wholly upon self assumed authority and without its knowledge. These are very numerous and of an outrageous character, fully in keeping with the treacherous negotiations conducted by him with Russia, reported in former despatches from this legation.

Upon the Korean Government's becoming aware of Von Mollendorff's negotiations with Russia through its discussions with the Russian Agent, M. de Speyer, a Korean Envoy was despatched to China to report his conduct to Li Hung Chang, the Viceroy of Chihli, by whom Von Möllendorff was placed originally in the service of the Korean Government. This Envoy returned to Korea on the 26th ultimo, and presented to the King, a report of charges against Von Möllendorff prepared by Li Hung Chang.

The conduct of this man would seem to be without a parallel in history. The audacity with which he originated and acted upon schemes of every sort, many of them involving the integrity of the state has been so bold as to create the impression far and wide that he was receiving the actual support of His Majesty, or controlled the powerful influence of the strong pro-Chinese faction in the Government. Nevertheless, I have long been aware that this was not actually the case; indeed, had even been informed by many nobles that his Majesty and the Government in general was wholly ignorant of the vast body of the work of Von Möllendorff, whom for sometime past they regarded suspiciously and with apprehension.

Prior to the revolutionary month of December last, Von Möllendorff was unquestionably the Agent of China, but was some what held in check by the more enlightened radical progressive patriots; these having been driven from the country, he began a most extraordinary and high-handed career. He openly denounced the conduct of several of the foreign representatives, more particularly that of the United States, the animus being the supervision by these legations authorities of contracts and schemes of several kinds with the Korean Government into which foreign merchants and others had been invited by him. In some cases these contracts were arranged without cognizance of the Legations, and such have invariably failed owing to the unscrupulous exactions of Von Möllendorff; and the outcome is that now a host of claims for exorbitant damages are being pushed against the Korean Government. Most of the schemes were wholly impracticable and failed wretchedly: for long times the foreign contracting parties have been restrained from vigorous actions for damages by promises of the most extraordinary sort made by Von Möllendorff.

I am pleased to state that, of the citizens and subjects of the several nationalities who have had dealings with Korea, Americans alone have suffered no pecuniary loss, none of these having been permitted to be seduced into the nefarious schemes presented and controlled by Von Möllendorff. However, I may report one case of controversy into which I have been forced with the Korean Government through Von Möllendorfs influence.

Two years ago nearly, the Chief of the Bureau of Colonization and improvement of Waste lands of Korea entered into a contract with the American Trading Company of Yokohama, Japan, by which the company was to cut, convey to Japan or China, and sell for a commission of ten per cent, the timber of a Korean Island called Ullonto. Later the company took the precaution to secure a second contract document from the same Bureau, and then having had Korean Officials sent to Ullonto about 20000 dollars worth of timber was cut and taken to Japan for sale.

The Chief of the Bureau of Colonization was Kim Ok Kiun, the leader of the conspiracy of December last. Though Von Mollendorff was perfectly aware of the existence of the American Company's contract no sooner had Kim been driven from the country after the December rioting in Seoul, than Von Mollendorff secured for an Englishman and a German firm jointly a contract to admit of their removing and selling the timber of Ullonto island. For a time, the Korean Government seems to have been in total ignorance of this. Von M. having prepared the contract wholly himself, using the seal of the Government Foreign Office. A little later, I was appealed to for assistance by the American Trading Company who wished the validity of their contract assured in order that they could sell the timber they had in Japan, and which had become difficult owing to reports that a German firm held the real contract for all the Ullonto timber. I conversed with the President of the Foreign Office in regard to the matter and while he at first maintained that Kim Ok Kiun's acts from his childhood up, of an official character, had become annulled by his having turned traitor, I secured his attention and a request to address him a letter on the subject.

Some time since, I wrote and sent the letter to the Foreign Office. I learned at once that the Foreign Office could not meet its agreements, and later, that my letter had been referred to Von Möllendorff to have him dictate its reply. The reply was duly received, over the seal of the Foreign Office, and the signature of its President. It was weak but unobjectionable in tone to the final clause which was a plain sentence of invective, namely "You should deal with Kim Ok Kiun about the matter." I at once demanded an explanation of this, and then returned the letter to the Foreign Office, stating that I refused to receive such a letter &c. I then made some inquiries and found that Von Möllendorff had been boasting of his having dictated this objectionable sentence.

The President of the Foreign Office came to see me promptly about the matter, evincing much anxiety. I talked very plainly to him, and he quickly apologised, saying Von M. had advised the use of the offensive clause. I insisted upon further satisfaction and immediately received an apology in writing and a request to accept a new letter in place of the objectionable one. This letter I accepted, and it proves highly satisfactory, indicating that the government will re-assure the validity of the American contract &c.

I then demanded that Von Möllendorff be dismissed from his office as adviser to the Foreign Office, as it was impossible for me to continue intercourse with that office so long as there was a chance of his being permitted to use puerile invective to vent his personal ill feelings by using the name of the government. This was promised and Von M's incapacity to direct official work of the Korean Government admitted. I was then told that Von M. had informed the Government that the American Trading Company had sold the Ullonoto timber in Japan and turned over the proceeds

Struggle for Control 123

to the traitor Kim Ok Kiun; that it was through having received this money that the conspirators had been able to support themselves in Japan—a falsehood without foundation and great malignity, which I controverted easily. With profound amazement the President of the Foreign Office learned that a credit of money remained to the Korean Government in the hands of the American Trading Company, and that it was decreasing constantly through loss of interest and unavailable because of the high handed conduct of Von Mollendorff. The result of the matter has been a degree of frankness and good feeling between this Legation and all factions of the Korean Government which has not heretofore existed, and a clear prospect of the contracts of the American Company being fully recognized as valid.

I have been aware that in this matter my action was of a character to suggest the propriety of its having first been submitted to the Department, but I deem the case to have been one in which prompt measures were to be used and much might be lost by waiting until the Department could be heard from.

I cannot here give all the undoubted and unquestionable authentic facts, well known in Korea at present tending to show the utter incapacity of Mr. Von Möllendorff to hold any office in this country by virtue of which he may be thrown into intercourse with foreign officials, and it is impossible for any of these to do other than to insist upon his removal from the service of the Korean Government.

George C. Foulk

NO. 212 August 6, 1885.

Secretary of State

Sir,

I have the honor to inform you that the Government of Korea has issued a notification to the effect that from August 3, 1885, contracts of every description made in the name of the Korean Government by Korean Officers, merchants and all other Korean subjects with foreign persons or foreign companies, must bear the seal of the Office for Foreign Affairs of Korea in order to be valid with, and as a sign of their having been authorized by the Government of Korea. Contracts not bearing the seal of the Foreign Office will not be recognized as Governmental, but as those of private individuals only.

This notification was sent to each of the Foreign representatives from the Foreign Office with a request that its substance be made known to the people of the several nationalities represented in Korea.

The Korean government has been much embarrassed heretofore through the making of contracts with foreigners by some of its nobles and officers in the name of the Government but without its knowledge or authority at the time. A number of troublesome cases of claims for damages is now before the Government on account of this practice: these have prompted the issue of the above notification.

In acknowledging the receipt of the notification I informed the Foreign Office of my assumption that it did not apply to contracts entered into prior to its date, by Korean Officers, in the name of the Government.

I shall at once transmit copies of the notification to the United States representatives in China and Japan, with the request that American merchants and others in those countries may be informed of it.

George C. Foulk

NO. 70   Department of State
Washington, D. C.

Ensign George C. Foulk, U.S.N.   September 22, 1885

Sir:

I have received your No. 211, of the 4th ultimo, relative to the dismissal of P. G. Möllendorf from the Corean Foreign Office, in which he has been acting as Vice-President and adviser with the title and rank of a Corean nobleman, in consequence of his alledged secret and unauthorized transactions with Russia.

While approving your prompt and energetic action in defending the threatened contract rights of American citizens, as perhaps justified under the peculiar circumstances described by your despatch, yet I should remark on general principels, that in such cases, the settled policy of the government is not to intervene officially. It is, however, gratifing to know that the most cordial relations exist between your Legation and the Government at Seoul.

James D. Porter
Acting Secretary

Struggle for Control

NO. 214 August 16, 1885.

Secretary of State

Sir,

On the 6th instant, I was informed from the palace that a telegraphic despatch had been sent by the Viceroy Li Hung Chang to summon for the service of Korea Mr. O. N. Denny, as advisor to the Foreign Office, and one other American, not named as Commissioner of Customs. This telegram was sent after a discussion between the Viceroy Li, and Min Yong Ik, and the Korean Ambassador reported in my No. 211, as having been despatched to China with charges against Mr. Von Möllendorff.

On the 8th instant, I received a request in writing from the President of the Korean Foreign Office to telegraph to the United States Government with the view of hastening the coming of the assistants asked from America. I called upon the Chinese Commissioner at once, and discovered that the request addressed me by the President of the Foreign Office was the result of a despatch from the Viceroy Li to the Chinese Commissioner here to have the coming of the Army instructors hastened.

On yesterday, I learned that the Viceroy Li had received a reply to his despatch, or a despatch, from the United States Government to the effect that the assistants could not come until Congress had taken action in the matter.

I have decided that there is nothing to warrant my again telegraphing to the United States Government, as requested by the President of the Foreign Office, and have given him an explanation to that effect.

The interest shown by the Chinese authorities in the speedy coming of the American Assistants and more particularly that of the Army instructors, is strongly and anxiously manifested, and is without doubt due to China's apprehensions of danger to her suzerainty of Korea, through a possible attempt of Russia to insist upon the validity of the negotiations conducted in the name of the Korean Government by Mr. Von Möllendorff. As I have already reported, the point of these upon which the Agent M. de Speyer opened his work here, was the employment of Russian Army Officers by Korea. It is now ascertained that the number of these officers proposed to be at once sent to Korea was sixty.

It is the commonly expressed opinion here that there will be at least a serious controversy between the Korean Government and the Russian Minister soon expected to arrive, upon the subject of Mr. Von Möllendorffs negotiations. The Russian Minister is to come with an escort of several men of war. His salary will be $10000, and judging from the establishment selected, his legation will be the most imposing one of Korea.

While it is stated emphatically by Koreans and Chinese that he must leave the service of Korea entirely, Mr. Von Möllendorff remains in Seoul as head of the custom's service. He is known to be in active correspondence with Russian authorities, this giving rise to considerable apprehension among the Koreans. His abrupt dismissal, it is feared by the Korean Government, might drive him into Russian employment where his treachery might work great harm. It has therefore been purposed that China remove him, giving him at least a temporary office in the Chinese custom's service.

An English Naval force yet remains in occupation of Port Hamilton, and no further correspondence between the English Minister at Peking and the Korean Government on the subject (other than that heretofore reported in full, has been held): While consultations on this subject are occasionally invited of the English Consul General here by the Korean authorities, the latter present their protests mildly, and apparently only show any decided interest at all in the matter for the value of its effect upon Russia, the designs of which, and the negotiations of Von Möllendorff, are used by the Consul General in meeting the protests of the Korean Government. It has been intimated to me by the English Consul-General that China has been apathetic in the matter of the occupation of Port Hamilton, through her anticipation of the designs of Russia, and also of France, upon the port.

While Japan was formerly highly active in using her influence in the affairs of Korea, since the treaty of April last with China, she has been apparently little more than a passive observer. The new Japanese legation, now being built, is small and insignificant. The representative is a Chargé d'Affaire ad. interim. There is much to indicate that Japan has greatly altered her policy in regard to Korea, yielding much to the Chinese claim of suzerainty.

There has been a report that the integrity of Japan was touched upon in the Von Möllendorff negotiations with Russia, as the status of Tsushima Islands, which formerly belonged to Korea, entered into them. It is a fact that recently a second battalion of soldiers was sent there by Japan and fortifications begun.

In its entire ignorance of international methods of treating questions like those now so seriously involving the integrity of the country, its utter weakness as regards physical force, and through its long continued close relations with China, it is but a natural consequence that Korea now becomes more directly under the control of China. The attitude of the latter is now very markedly that of a sovereign state to its complete dependency.

I may mention that at a dinner given at the Chinese legation on the 8th instant in honor of the birthday of the Emperor of China, an address was read by the Commissioner in which it was stated "Korea is to China as lips to the teeth, and (being thus members of one body) each must share the joys and sorrows of the other." At this dinner the President of the Office for Foreign Affairs of Korea, the highest Korean in rank present and with whom the foreign representatives may deal, was placed at table after all the foreign representatives, two of whom were Consuls-General. In reply to a question I asked the Commissioner in regard to this unusual position of the President of the Foreign Office, he stated, that on such an occasion, the President was not a guest, but a member of the house of China. The Commissioner has since expressed to me that he regards his position under China, in Korea, as the equivalent of the *Resident* under England, in India.

A telegraph line is about to be constructed from Seoul, Korea to Peking, China, the route to be overland, via Mūkden. A danish Company has secured the contract for the work from China, and now has a surveying party at work in Korea.

I am aware that I have in this lengthy despatch, touched upon many points, each of which might have been more clearly presented in a separate despatch. But it has seemed to me there might be an advantage in having these in a collective form for use in the considerations pertaining to Korea, the Department may now have before it; it is in such a form, therefore, that I would now respectfully submit them.

George C. Foulk

NO. 215.　　　　　　　　　　*Confidential*　　　　　　　　August 17, 1885.

Secretary of State

Sir,

On the 15th instant, a Chinese vessel of war, the "Yangwei," was despatched from Chemulpho to Chefoo, China, bearing two Korean officers of rank, who, I am authoritatively informed, carry a commission from His Majesty the King to Min Yong Ik, by which he becomes General, Commander-in-Chief of the four Palace guard battalions. These Envoys also carry a tablet from His Majesty which makes the summons to Min Yong Ik urgent and imperative, and he must return to Korea with the utmost despatch.

This event is one of considerable significance in its bearing upon the internal conditions of affairs of the Korean Government and the relations of China and Korea.

Min Yong Ik held the office of Comdr-in-Chief of the Palace battalions at the time of his attempted assassination in December last, and the office is one of the highest in the Kingdom, carrying with it the voice of a Minister of State in the Royal cabinet. While holding this office he was in the more important parts of his work unquestionably responsible to and directed by the Chinese General then here in command of the Chinese troops, and from whom he received constant support, this during the revolutionary trouble and for several months thereafter, extending to the guard of his person by a considerable force of Chinese soldiers. Min Yong Ik, while a Korean by birth, and the title of his office, has always been and is today, practically a loyal Chinese Official, living up to the traditions of his family—that of the Queen,—which is the tie which binds Korea to China, or it may be said, the powerful wedge of Chinese interference in the affairs of Korea.

Through the beheading of his father in December last, Min Yong Ik is now the head of his family, and the most powerful noble in Korea; indeed, as supported by the Chinese, practically in matters of State intimately, and including foreign relations as well, must under the present circumstances, exceed that of the Sovereign; and this authority does not necessarily depend upon any actual office he may hold under the King of Korea.

The present installation of Min Yong Ik as Commander-in-Chief is to be traced directly to Chinese dictation, and has for its direct object the placing of the capital troops of Korea under the direction of the Chinese authorities in Seoul as a precaution against intrigues of the Tai-wen-kun, the presumable enemy of China and the Mins now as he was at the time he directed the revolt of 1882 against the latter. This would imply the earlier return of the Tai-wen-kun to Korea than I expected at the time of addressing the Department in my despatch No. 206, since which I have learned that his being returned to Korea by China is an imperative result of the recent conference between China and Japan.

For some time past there have been many rumors current in Seoul to the effect that Kim Ok Kiun, the radical progressivist leader of the revolutionary attempt of December last, was endeavoring to effect his return to Korea from Japan for the purpose of leading the supposed remainder of his party yet in Korea in further attempts at accomplishing the objects of the December conspiracy. I am assuredly aware that he has been active in Japan, as has been shown by his attempts to consult with certain foreign

Struggle for Control

representatives there, and correspondence I know of his constantly maintaining with Koreans, some of them in high official positions in Korea.

Korean officers of rank have repeatedly come to me with anxious questions as to what I had heard of Kim Ok Kiun's conduct in Japan, and expressing the fear that he might attach a number of Japanese, known to be in sympathy with him, to his cause, and secretly enter Korea again where he might be joined by other members of his party in an attempt to overthrow the government.

The apprehension in regard to Kim Ok Kiun's intentions has been augmented within the past few days by considerations of the return of the Tai-wen-kun. From the foregoing it will be seen that the supposed political views of the Tai-wen-kun and those of Kim Ok Kiun are the same, both have been fatal enemies of the Mins and Chinese rule in Korea. To the Government, there is therefore the possibility of Kim Ok Kiun's timing the fulfillment of his designs against the government by the return of the Tai-wen-kun, with whom he may make common cause. Apprehension of this has prompted the government to take steps to examine hereafter all persons arriving by steamers and other vessels at Chemulpho.

Unquestionably much of this apprehension is due to suspicion of Japan, which Koreans of almost every class believe to be in sympathy with Kim Ok Kiun and to have given aid to his attempt in December last. This unfriendly suspicion has been openly expressed to me also by the Chinese officer's here.

It will have been shown by this communications and my No. 214, that Korea has of necessity become more assuredly than heretofore under the control of China, also that attempts to reverse this position are possible. However, the pro-offered protection of China has been asked for and voluntarily accepted, though there are evidences that this was done with reluctance on the part of His Majesty.

George C. Foulk

59   18 August 1885

George C. Foulk

Sir:

I have received and read with interest your Confidential despatch No. 186 of June 23rd last, in regard to the secret negotiations of the P. G. von Möllendorf, for Corea, with Russia.

In this connection, I desire to advert to the conclusion of your despatch suggesting that the Chinese and Japanese troops should remain longer in Corea, and to remind you that very great discretion is necessary in making such intimations to the Chinese and Japanese representatives. The Government of the United States has no concern in these matters beyond that of a friendly State which has treated with Corean as independent and Sovereign and hopes to see her position as such among nations assured.

T. F. Bayard

NO. 224.   Sept. 2, 1885.

Secretary of State

Sir,

I would respectfully report that for several months past, the Korean Government has been taking active steps towards the improvement of its military force, and more particularly, to have it in such shape that the expected Military instructors may upon their arrival, promptly begin their work of rendering it practically efficient after Western military tactics.

Some time since, an order—with an advance payment of $8000.—was given the American Trading Company of Yokohama, Japan, to furnish His Majesty with 6 new model Gatling guns and 75000 cartridges: these are expected to arrive from the United States at an early date. In regard to these guns, an order for them was given last year by His Majesty to the Gatling Gun Company of Hartford, Conn.; the order was suppressed however, in January last by Mr. P. G. Von Möllendorff, who had formerly offered to procure them at a cost of $7000 apiece, while the price of the 6 guns and 75000 cartridges ordered by his Majesty was fairly fixed at $16000—delivered at Chemulpho, Korea.

Orders have also been given for a supply of powder, caps and bullets, with a number of reloading machines, these to be used in reloading shells expended in practice already with the 3000 Remington and 1000 Peabody-Martini rifles now in the hands of the troops. 200000 cartridges have also been ordered and the purchase of powder making machinery is under consideration.

The troops of the capital guard are the only ones of Korea which have as yet been organized with considerations of Western methods. They are divided into four battalions and number about 4000 men. They have been

Struggle for Control

well exercised in the use of modern rifles by long continued target practice; are uniformed, well garrisoned, and subordinate; but are sadly deficient in training as to the manual of arms, company or platoon drill, or fighting tactics. The officers are Koreans of the old civilization without any knowledge of the requirements of troops to be trained after Western methods.

In regard to the supplies for the troops referred to above I may state that their being ordered is the outcome of requests for advice on the subject to which they pertain made to me last year, and to which I responded as authorized by the instructions issued to me as Naval Attaché to this Legation.

George C. Foulk

NO. 231.   Legation of the United States
Seoul, Korea.
Sept. 25, 1885.

Secretary of State

Sir,

I have the honor to inform the Department of State that a Commissioner of Telegraphs, despatched by China, has arrived in Korea, and with a force of workmen consisting of foreigners of a Danish telegraph Company and Chinese, is now actively engaged in erecting a line of telegraph of considerable extent in this country.

The line will begin at Chemulpho thence go to Seoul, whence it will be extended northward through Peng Yang, the capital of Phyöng An, the northwest province of Korea, to Oichū (I Chow in Chinese), a town of Korea on the Amnot River (Yalu, in Chinese): at the latter place, the line will connect with the telegraph extending from Peking through Mukden

Upon close inquiry of officers of the Korean Government, I learn that this telegraph line is to be built under an agreement entered into by Korea with China, according to which, China is to erect the line, furnishing the whole of the money required, and to establish it in working order. Korea is to receive all the receipts of the line during the first five years of its operation, and to pay no money to China on account of the cost of the line during that interval: during each of twenty years subsequent to the expiration of these five years, Korea will pay to China five thousand taels. At the end of twenty-five years, the line is to become the sole property of the Korean

Government. The total cost of the line in money to be paid to China by Korea will therefore be, one hundred thousand taels.

By the present highways, the distance from Chemulpho to Oichū, via Seoul, is about 370 miles, while the length of the line will be less than this distance, it will probably be less shortened than a telegraph line over similar land in Western countries would be, on account circuitous routes it may be made to take in consideration of the superstitions of the people in regard to graves, dwellings &c.

There will be four offices of the line in Korea; namely at Chemulpho, Seoul (Han Söng), Peng Yang, and Oichū. At these the operators are to be furnished by China, and at each office will be Korean students, these being under the direction of an inferior Korean Officer, who has studied telegraphy in Japan and is the chief representative for Korean interests in the line.

On the 11th instant, there appeared posted in the most conspicuous places in Seoul, a proclamation of the Chinese Commissioner of Telegraphs; a copy of the translation of this I enclose. This document has excited comment, as to the character of which I need not remark upon. It is in keeping with the tenor of all Chinese official dealings with this country.

The manner of conducting the arrangements for this telegraph line has given special dissatisfaction to Japan, and its establishment by the Chinese has been represented to the Korean Government as an infringement upon rights given Japan by Korea in an agreement entered into and concerning telegraphs, made at the time the Japanese submarine cable was laid from Nagasaki, Japan to Fusan in Korea.

The establishment of this line of telegraph to connect the Korean capital with Peking, is unquestionably based upon political motives; and though the proclamation of the Commissioner of Telegraphs states that the erection of it by China was requested of Li Hung Chang, the Chinese Superintendent of Northern Trade, by the King of Korea, by close questioning and observation I can discover but that the King and Government of Korea had little or no independent action in the matter at all.

The Chinese, suspicious of Russian designs upon Korea to an unusual degree through the recent negotiations of Mr. Von Möllendorff, and the work of the Russian Agent M. de Speyer, which I have reported in full to the Department, and suspicious as well of the Koreans themselves, realize the necessity of keeping a closer surveillance over political and military affairs of the Korean capital than heretofore: this it decided to effect by the telegraphic bond, the Korean side of which in all probability is meant to

Struggle for Control 133

be the Chinese "Commissioner of Trade," or other Chinese representative in Seoul, rather than the King of Korea or his Government.

It is expected that the telegraph line will be open to Peking within sixty days, and work is being pushed upon it with much vigor.

George C. Foulk

NO. 237. Oct. 14, 1885.

Secretary of State

Sir,

I have the honor to report that on the 3d instant, a Chinese vessel of war arrived at Chemulpho, Korea bearing the Tai-Wön-Kun, ex-Regent and father of His Majesty, the King of Korea, who was taken to China by force in 1882 and has since been retained there by the Chinese Government.

The possible return of the Tai Wön Kun has for some time been the subject of much speculation and has excited wide interest in the East. However, no exact or possible date for his return to Korea would seem to have been fixed, or at least been intimated to the public, or the Government of Korea. His arrival therefore at Chemulpho on the 3d instant was a sudden surprise in Korea.

The news of the arrival spread with great rapidity, and by the morning of the 4th instant, some 7–8000 natives of Seoul had assembled at Chemulpho to welcome him. The Government despatched but one officer of high rank, and His Majesty was represented by two of the principal eunuchs of the Palace.

The duty of escorting the Tai Wön Kun to Korea was intrusted to the Chinese General Yuen, who commanded the Chinese troops prior to and during the emeute in Seoul of December last.

On the 5th instant the Tai Wön Kun was conducted to Seoul under a guard of forty Chinese Marines and followed by the multitude of people who had gone to Chemulpho to welcome him. At the Great South Gate of Seoul, a temporary pavillion had been erected; in this, to which he had proceeded in State, screened from public gaze, the King met his aged father. The streets of Seoul were thronged during the day by excited multitudes of people. From the pavillion, the King returned to the Palace, and the Tai Wön Kun was escorted by the Chinese to his former residence.

The general expression of the people over the return of the Tai Wön Kun is one of joy, mingled with apprehension evinced in many ways. Among the officers of the Government anxiety amounting almost to consternation is evinced; numbers of these, and some of the people as well left the city, and the offices of the Government were half deserted and inactive for several days following the arrival.

A most unfortunate occurrence in its effect upon the already excited state of the Government and people took place by the Queen's order on the 5th and 6th instants, in the execution of three persons charged with having aided the Tai Won Kun's attempt of three years ago upon the life of the Queen. The 9th ultimo was the anniversary of the return of the Queen to Seoul after the attempt of the Tai Wön Kun in 1882, during which she was supposed to have been poisoned, but had escaped to the country. The Anniversary was celebrated in the palace by a grand dinner and a series of games, to which the foreign representatives were invited—and attended, though not without some mis-givings. On this date, the Queen effected the beginning of a fresh system—after a lapse of over three years—of ferretting out persons supposed to have aided in the Tai Wön Kun's attempt of 1882. By the 5th instant, the prisons were well filled with suspects, whose names had been divulged under the severe torture applied to the first few arrested.

The three executions above referred to were timed to the arrival of the Tai Wön Kun with the evident object of intimidating the people against giving him new support in their enthusiasm over his return. This action the foreign representatives openly criticised to the Government as one tending only to increase public danger and excitement. On the 9th instant the Chinese General Yön took steps and prevented further executions, and the dismembered bodies of the executed persons were removed from the streets in which they had been lying.

As might be expected these executions have had the effect of placing the people in a deplorable state of excitement and apprehension. The Chinese however, have taken pains to cause it to be known that no further executions would be allowed, and now the excitement is waning... [remainder of MS illegible]

George C. Foulk

Struggle for Control 135

NO. 240 Oct. 15, 1885

Secretary of State

Sir:

I have to report that the present Chinese Commissioner for Trade in Seoul is about to be recalled, to be succeeded by the Chinese General Yuen, mentioned in my No. 237 as having arrived in Korea on the 3rd instant with the Tai Won Kun.

The appointment of General Yuen to the post of Commissioner of Trade in Seoul is significant in view of the attitude he maintained in Korea prior to and during the revolutionary attempt of December last in Seoul when he commanded the Chinese forces here. He is a young man, vigorous and active, and received honors from the Viceroy Li Hung Chang as one of the latter's most trusted and efficient servants.

In my despatch No. 215 dated August 17, I have stated to the effect that prior to the troubles of December last, General Yuen was the actual commander of both the Chinese and Korean troops in Seoul. There yet remain in Seoul many tablets erected by the people to honor General Yuen for the steps he took in December to overthrow the government of the conspirators.

In his call upon me General Yuen referred to the coming of M. O. N. Denny to Korea to serve as advisor to the Korean Government and took occasion to remark with positiveness that if Mr. Denny came here on summons of China, he, the General, would cause Korea to implicitly follow his advice.

This remark was extraordinary to me in that it was the first positive utterance of a Chinese official I have heard to the effect that China would not permit Korea to be free in her foreign and internal affairs. Nevertheless it has long been apparent to me that China controls Korea with an oppressive and a strong hand.

George C. Foulk

NO. 243 20 October 1885

Secretary of State

Sir:

In accordance with the customs of official etiquette in this country, I have asked for and had an audience with the Tai Wön Kun, ex-Regent and father of the King of Korea reported in my No. 237 as recently having been returned from China by the Chinese Government.

The audience was held in the private residence—a small palace—of the Tai Wön Kun. The Tai Wön Kun received me with pleasing dignity on the steps of the Audience chamber, and taking me by the hand, led me within where a light collation was prepared.

I found the Tai Won Kun a very remarkably well preserved man, sixty-eight years old, but appearing to be not more than fifty. His face shows great decision and firmness, with high intelligence. He is active in speech and motion of body.

The conversation was frank and agreeable. He stated that he was not civilized in the Western way, that he had lived in seclusion in China and had met only one or two foreigners when there; that he had been advised to lead a life of retirement in Korea, content with the honor done him as King of Korea. He asked me many questions—a few touching upon political affairs and to which I replied as guardedly as possible. When I withdrew he stated that he was old and lame, and possibly would not return my call and asked me to come often informally to see him.

However, the Tai Wön Kun returned my call on the 11th instant, together with the calls of the other foreign representatives who had asked for audience with him. During the call he stated the Chinese and the King did not wish him to use his name, but the simple title Tai Wön Kun (Great Prince of the Royal House). As he was leaving the legation I overheard him say to one of my head servants "Remember always that you are a Korean, and do all you can to help your country, though you serve in a foreign house."

The result of my observation is that I believe the Tai Wön Kun is a man who cannot, with his present strength and activity of mind avoid being drawn into active participation in the affairs of the government.

The Chinese authorities treat him with great deference and kindliness, and without doubt it has been their endeavor to cause him to lean towards their policy in Korea. However they show much anxiety and are vigilently watching him.

The Tai Wön Kun has been the deadly enemy of the Queen's house, which has endeavored by every possible means to prevent his return to Korea.

The Queen and her family are fearful of his further intriguing against them, and a breach has occurred between them and the Chinese over the latters having returned him to Korea; by this a new phase of Korean

Struggle for Control 137

politics is presented, the whole power of the Queen's party heretofore having been dependent upon its happy relations with and the unwavering support given by China.

It is possible that the Chinese have already observed that the Tai Wön Kun cannot remain inactive in Korea, and that he may endeavor to release Korea from their oppressive interference; for yesterday an envoy started for China with a request from the Korean Government for the stationing of Chinese troops in Seoul—a request most reasonably inferred as having been dictated by the Chinese themselves.

George C. Foulk

NO. 255   *Confidential*   Nov. 25, 1885

Secretary of State

Sir:

In my No. 240, dated Oct. 15, 1885, I reported that General Yuen was about to become the Commissioner for China in Seoul. Shortly after making the above dispatch, General Yuen together with the late Commissioner for China, Chen Shu Fang, went to Tientsin—these officials have just returned to Korea and General Yuen has taken over charge of the duties of the chief representative of China in Korea.

On the 18th instant I received a notification from the President of the Korean office for Foreign Affairs in which it is stated that H. E. Yuen is dispatched to Korea to assume charge of the Diplomatic and Commercial intercourse, with a title much higher than that of the late Commissioner for China.

On the 19th instant an assistant of the Chinese representative, a young Chinese who was educated in the United States called upon me to deliver the card of H. E. Yuen, and to explain that H. E. would call upon me after he should have had audience with the King. I asked this gentleman if the expression "Charge of Diplomatic and Commercial intercourse" used in the notification of the President of the Foreign Office of Korea, signified that the grade of H. E. Yuen was Minister Resident; to this the assistant replied promptly, "Oh no, China cannot give the title of Minister to its representatives in Seoul, for that would be for China to admit the independence of Korea." "What then," I inquired, "would be the exact title of H. E. Yuen in English?" "Resident," the assistant replied. The card of

H. E. Yuen handed me by the assistant bore three characters of the name, in Chinese and, in English, the words, "H. I. C. M. Resident" Seoul".

I would, at this point, ask reference to No. 214, dated August 16, 1885 in which I have reported the remarks of the late Chinese Commissioner, Chen Shu Fang, upon his position at a dinner given by him on the birthday of the Emperor of China.

On the 20th instant, Mr. Baber, Consul General for England, and Mr. Takahira Kogoro, chargé d'affairs ad interim for Japan, called upon me to discuss the title and rank of Mr. Yuen, the new Chinese representative. The latter officer showed much interest and some anxiety. Neither of these gentlemen had had Mr. Yuen's positions explained to them as "Resident" nor had received the card above described. Both had observed, however, that Mr. Yuen's title and grade were higher than those of his predecessor, as given in the notification of the President of the Foreign Office of Korea, but were unable to fix, in English, an English title to correspond to the description, "to take charge in Korea of Diplomatic and Commerical Intercourse." In my acknowledgement of receipt of the notification of the Foreign Office, I referred to Mr. Yuen's title by the translation, "Commissioner with Diplomatic Powers." The English Consul General has since used the title "Resident Commissioner" in his translations. Both Mr. Takahira and Mr. Baber expressed the opinion that the question of the title and functions of Mr. Yuen was a great one in its bearing on the conditions and understandings under which the treaties had been made with Korea.

On the 21st instant Mr. P. G. Von Mollendorff had a farewell audience with the King of Korea. On the following day, a Korean officer told me that as he was taking leave of the King on the 21st Mr. von Mollendorff remarked to the effect that the appointment by China of General Yuen boded ill for Korea, and advised His Majesty in case of difficulty in dealing with him as Chinese representative, to refer questions to the Foreign representatives.

On the 23rd instant Mr. Yuen called upon me. Believing that the question of an advisor for Korea had some bearing on the increased rank of the Chinese representative, I inquired if Mr. O. N. Denny had accepted China's summons to become the advisor to the Korean Government. Mr. Yuen replied that Mr. Denny would not come to Korea. "That having been settled upon," I remarked, "what would China next do in way of providing an advisor for Korea?" Mr. Yuen replied that China did not wish an advisor for Korea at present, and none would be invited: that in compliance

Struggle for Control 139

with a request of the King of Korea, he (General Yuen), had been appointed to this post in Korea, and he would be the advisor to the King and government, assisted by the foreign representatives whom he would consult. Mr. Yuen went on to state that he had been specially instructed to maintain warm relations with the United States representative in Seoul, and requested me, with seeming earnestness, to assist him by consultation, adding that he was not familiar with diplomatic usages.

I then referred to the title written upon his card, asking if he was to be regarded as "Resident" in the sense of that word as applied to the English official who resides with the Rajahs and other native chiefs of state in the Residences of India. To this question Mr. Yuen did not give a direct reply but instead, a general one to the effect that the King of Korea would submit questions of state to him, and he would consult with the other foreign representative, particularly myself. China, he stated, wished to be guided largely by the United States in Korean matters, and this desire had already been emphasized by the summons by China to Mr. Denny, the appointment of Mr. Merrill to manage the customs of Korea, and the invitation to the United States Government to furnish military instructors for Korea. I replied by saying that these were flattering to my government and no doubt highly appreciated by it.

On yesterday, a Korean officer came to me from the Palace, stating that he had been sent by his Majesty the King to ask questions in regard to the coming of an advisor for Korea. He stated that when some time since, a Korean envoy was sent to China with a communication from the King to the Viceroy Li in regard to Mr. von Möllendorff's negotiations with Russia (I refer to it in No. 214 dated August 16, 1885), this envoy was instructed by the King to telegraph to the U. S. Government to effect the speedy coming of an advisor for Korea, and the military instructors. This envoy, instead of acting himself, committed his instructions to the Viceroy Li (It is significant that at this time *Min* Yong Ik was in Tientsin and has been mentioned, as reported in my No. 214 dated August 16, 1885, as a party to a discussion upon the subject of an advisor and military officers for Korea). China acted at once upon the information given by the envoy, telegraphed respecting the coming of the military instructors, and made her choice of Mr. Denny as advisor and summoned him by telegram. (It was not until several weeks had elapsed that the King of Korea knew that China had selected Mr. Denny to become the advisor to his government.)

The King was content with the prospect of Mr. Dennys becoming his advisor, after, upon questioning, he had learned that he was an American of excellent standing and superior qualifications. (In this connection I may state pertinently that some time ago a Korean officer came to me from the Palace to ask whether if Mr. Denny came here, he would serve China or Korea!) The officer from his Majesty went on to state that as it was now known that Mr. Denny would not come to Korea upon the summons of China, His Majesty was now considering the framing of a fresh request to the United States Government to have it select for him an advisor for his government!—and my opinion on this subject was asked by his Majesty.

I replied that I could not well remark upon this subject, beyond that in view of the peculiar relations of Korea, China and Japan at this time, it might prove embarrassing to any government to entertain such a request; and also that as to obtain an advisor through any government much time would necessarily be required; it would perhaps be better if His Majesty's government were to invite directly some competent person to come as Advisor.

The above narrative well illustrates the embarrassing position in which I am constantly being placed in Korea, and I may trust, will show how great the necessity for my being most explicitly instructed by the government. Because I am able to communicate with Koreans perhaps more readily than other foreign representatives here, and of my long residence in Korea, and the very favor in which I stand with a large body of the leading officials, I am forced into a prominence hardly commensurate with such prudence and far-sightedness as I may have acquired in my short experience in diplomatic duty.

George C. Foulk

260   Decr. 9, 1885

Secretary of State

Sir:

I have the honor to report, with reference to the contents of my despatch No. 255 dated Nov. 25, that the Chinese representative has informed me that Mr. O. N. Denny in acceptance of the summons of China, is now on his way to China and will arrive in Korea on or about the first of January—to serve as Adviser to the Korean Government.

Struggle for Control   141

In replying to my questions on this subject addressed me by Korean officers of the King's party, I have deemed it proper to discourage efforts to obtain another adviser than Mr. Denny by addressing the United States Government. I now learn that his Majesty will be pleased to receive Mr. Denny.

George C. Foulk

265   Confidential   December 29, 1885

Secretary of State

Sir:

On the 13th instant two Korean officers in their court robes came to me late in the afternoon, saying they had been sent by His Majesty to ask my opinion in regard to an expedition said to have left Japan under the direction of Kim Ok Kiun (the leader in the conspiracy of December last year) to come to Korea. They stated that his Majesty had been informed by the Chinese representative that the latter had received a telegram on that date (13th Decr.) from the Chinese Minister in Japan, stating that Kim Ok Kiun had sailed from Shimonoseki, Japan, in company with a company of renegade Japanese in eight Japanese junks, ostensibly bound for a Japanese port, and in ballast, but in reality bound for Korea and carrying a quantity of arm and ammunition. This news, the officers stated, was causing much excitement and apprehension among the nobles and officers of the Government.

I could only say to these officers that I had received no news on the subject, and thought there were no ground for apprehension; also that there was probably some mistake, and that it was not likely that Japan would permit the departure of such an expedition.

Late, on the same day, Mr. Baber, the British Consul-General called and stated as follows, showing some excitement. He had called that afternoon at the Chinese Legation and was there read a telegram which had just been received by the Chinese representative from the Chinese Minister in Japan, giving the information to the exact effect of the news in regard to Kim Ok Kiun's expedition I had heard from the Palace officers, and above (reported) noted. The Chinese representative stated that he had telegraphed to the Viceroy Li Hung Chang, suggesting that Chinese vessels of war be sent to patrol the coast of Korea; that he feared Kim Ok Kiun might land, or had landed already, and with his armed followers; would call an additional force of Koreans and approach Seoul. Mr. Baber questioned the Chinese representative as to the propriety of at once making this news known to the Japanese representative, but to this Mr. Yuan dissented. Mr. Baber had telegraphed to the British representative in Peking the substance of the Chinese telegram and asked for a gunboat to be sent to Chemulpho.

Mr. Baber later saw the Japanese (~~representative~~) chargé d'affairs during the evening, and learned he had received no news from his government of Kim Ok Kiun's expedition.

I told Mr. Baber of what I had heard, and stated that I did not believe it possible that Japan would permit the departure ~~and~~ or fitting out of such an expedition; and further that it would be most extraordinary if while the Chinese minister in Japan should have become aware of the fitting out and departure of such an expedition the Japanese Government should be in ignorance of it.

On the following day, again I was asked for information from the Palace, and was told, in answer to my inquiries, that the Korean Government had been advised not to refer to the Japanese Chargé d'affairs, upon the subject of the expedition, by the Chinese representative, who had telegraphed for further information.

On the 15th instant, an English gunboat arrived at Chemulpho from Chefoo, followed by another a few days later. Three Chinese gunboats also appeared there. I wrote a note to the commanding officer of the U. S. S. "Marion" at Chemulpho, to inform him of what had happened and particularly to dispell the impressions left upon him by exaggerated stories and rumors he might have heard at that port.

During the evening of the 15th instant, an officer came from the Palace to say that the Chinese representative had received a second telegram from the Chinese Minister in Tokyo, saying that Kim Ok Kiun had meant to sail for Korea with an armed force, but his intentions having become known to the Chinese Minister, the latter had caused the Japanese Government, through its Foreign Office, to seize Kim and his confederates. The officer from the Palace stated that there were doubts to His Majesty as to what had actually occurred in Japan, and he had been directed by His Majesty to ask me to telegraph to Japan for details. To this I replied that it was beyond my province and instructions to take any part in such a matter and that it was one which could properly be treated of only in Seoul, by consulting the representatives of Japan here.

Struggle for Control

On the 16th instant, I received a lengthy telegram in cipher preceded by the following words,

"Foulke, U.S. Chargé d'Affairs, Seoul-Corea per telegraph from ,(Tientsin) please transmit the following telegram to Japanese Chargé d'Affairs and get the reply and wire to me. Irwin, hawaiian chargé d'affairs (Tokio)." After some deliberation I sent the telegram to the Japanese Chargé d'Affairs with a note stating that I would prefer not to transmit the reply as requested in the telegram, unless it proved to be absolutely necessary for me to have to do so on business of my Government.

I have reason to believe that by this telegram in cipher the Japanese representative received his first intimation as to what had occurred in Japan, and upon which the Chinese telegrams had been based. Mr. Irwin, who had sent it, is the Hawaiian Chargé d'affairs in Tokio, but I was aware that he has long occupied a position as Confidential Agent or Advisor to the Japanese Government.

On the 18th instant, a second telegram addressed me by Mr. Irwin, requested me to inform him as to whether his previous telegram had been delivered. I informed the Japanese Chargé of this, and asked an explanation of my being used as a medium of communication between himself and his government. An attaché of the Japanese Legation was sent to say that as there were questions open between Corea and Japan in regard to telegraph lines, the Japanese Government could not openly patronize the Chinese line from Seoul to Peking; the Japanese Chargé d'Affairs requested my good offices as had been asked in Mr. Irwin's telegram.

I called upon the Japanese Chargé d'Affairs at once, and with an explanation of my reasons for not acceding to his request, declined to communicate for him with Mr. Irwin and his Government. I am convinced that it is my duty not to take the smallest part in any controversy, or correspondence likely to lead to such, between the Governments of Japan, China and Korea, in which the United States is not clearly and directly concerned.

It has been intimated that the Chinese telegrams are based upon the arrest by the Japanese Government, in November last, of a number of low Japanese who were suspected of designs to enter Korea and there create difficulties which should lead to war between China and Japan. As yet there is no published evidence that the Korean conspirators in Japan have had any part in the movement of these low Japanese. To say the least, the conduct of the Chinese representatives in Japan and Korea is greatly to be deplored. The effects of the despatches transmitted by them, and of having made their contents broadly known, can only be to humble Korea and tend to cause her, out of fear of Japan particularly, and all other nations than China in general as well, to shrink Chinawards—to become but a jealously guarded outlying province of that country.

George C. Foulk

NO. 26.
Secretary of State

Legation of the United States
Seoul, Korea
Aug. 25, 1886

Sir:

There has been great excitement in this city for the last ten days in consequence of the banishment of four officers of the Home Depart. on the 16th inst.

It was understood a few days after that this action of the King was at the Instigation of Mr. Youen, the Chinese Minister whose course here has been a very domineering one.

On the 20th inst. Min Yong Ik, who is understood to be in the interests of China, sailed for that country in a Chinese Gunboat.

The excitement still existing in Seoul and the leading American citizens feeling somewhat anxious, I wrote Captain McGlensey of the Ossipee to return to Chemolpo, which he did yesterday the 24th, inst.

A few hours after he arrived a Chinese Gunboat and six Transports with troops arrived at the same place. Upon this I telegraphed Capt. McGlensey to send from the Ossipee a guard of twenty men to protect the Legation which he promises to do tomorrow.

It is impossible to foretell what the next action of the Chinese Government will be, though it looks to me very much as if China intends to assert her rights to the protectorate of Korea.

As by the Treaty made the spring of 1885, between China and Japan, both parties agreed to withdraw their troops from Korea and not land there again. Any further activity on the part of the Chinese would be likely to bring on a war between those two countries.

The mail for the U. S. closes today but I will take the advantage of every opportunity to keep the Depart. informed of matters here.

Wm. H. Parker

Struggle for Control

NO. 31   Dip. Series   Department of State,
Washington, August 18, 1886

Wm H. Parker, Esqr.

Seoul

Sir:

I enclose, for your information, a copy of a despatch from Mr. Chas. Denby, United States Minister in China, No. 156, of the 5th ultimo, with its printed accompaniment, purporting to give the advice of Li Hung Chang to the government of Corea respecting the latter's relations toward Russia.

T. F. Bayard

NO. 156.   Legation of the United States
Peking July 5th 1886.

Secretary of State

Washington, D. C.

Sir:

I have the honor to forward to you herewith, for your information, an extract from a Shanghai newspaper purposing to give the substance of a memorial addressed by Li Hung Chang to the King of Corea on the policy which he should adopt toward the Russians in view of the frontiers of the two countries being conterminous.

Charles Denby

China and Corea

Memorial addressed by Hi Lung Chang to the King of Corea upon the negotiations with Russia.

I desire with great respect to present to Your Majesty some observations, in the form of questions and answers, upon the advantages and disadvantages which may arise from commercial transactions on the frontier, between Corea and Russia.

1st Q. Are the frontiers of Corea and Corea conterminous, and what distance separates the two frontiers?

A. As far as 20 *li* from the mouth of the river Tomen the left bank is the Russian frontier, and the right the Corean. Beyond that the river forms the boundary of Kirin.

2nd Q. Since the frontier between Russia and Corea extends for 20 *li* from the mouth of the river, is it necessary to establish commercial relations on that frontier?

A. If the frontier extended 1,000 *li* it would certainly be well to establish commercial transactions as they are a source of wealth to the people, but the frontier only extending 20 *li* the coast trade suffices and frontier transactions need not be authorized.

3rd Q. If Russia tried to force her projects by arms on the frontier what would you do?

A. As the treaties recently signed between Corea and other countries are commercial ones only, if Russia tried to force a treaty with her, she would be in the wrong, and the other treaty powers have authority to decide who is in the right.

4th Q. Have the Russians any other object in trying to establish commercial relations on the frontier, or not?

A. Commerce between Russia and Corea being so small, Russia certainly has another aim in view. One can easily see the disadvantages following their project. Duties coud not be collected on the frontier so well as by the Customs. Would those bringing merchandise up the T'omen in ships be considered as land or sea traders? There being only one barrier on that frontier it would be very difficult to stop smuggling.

5th Q. What is the chief aim the Russians have?

A. They mean to encroach on Corea on the slightest quarrel. A land trade is certain to raise many quarrels and it is better for Corea to have no land trade at all.

6th Q. What is the best means of avoiding a quarrel between the two nations?

A. The three principal causes of frontier quarrels are:

(1) Building forts and stationing troops on the frontier.

(2) Receiving fugitives and hiding them in the interior.

(3) Receiving fugitives from neighboring countries and naturalizing them.

The law of nations forbid the building of forts on the frontiers. There are between all nations laws of extradition, and criminals, the worst of whom are those who incite rebellion, should be handed over to their authorities. Unless Corea makes a law of extradition with Russia, then there will arise many causes of quarrel. Even if Corea made such a law with Russia, it would not be kept by Russia in the same as by the Corean Government, for at present there are two parties in Corea, Conservative and Progressive. These parties profiting by frontier trade will pass over the frontier, and there with impunity will await favorable oppurtunities, therefore the first thing Corea would have to do would be to establish barriers on the frontier to examine all those who wish to pass. Law permits men to change their nationality, and Russia would eagerly seize poor Coreans to people their vast plains, saying they were doing them good.

7th Q. O what importance to China is the establishing of a frontier trade between Russia and Corea?

A. As the boundary of China next these two countries is only 20 *li* from the mouth of the T'omen an able Commissioner would have to be sent at once to reside there, delimit it and guard it. If this was neglected it would be useless where once the Russians had commenced their encroachments.

As the question of frontier commerce is of the greatest importance, I shall be happy if Your Majesty will give a little of your attention to what I have written under the form of a conversation between two persons.

Following these questions and answers are some remarks and advice from Li Hung Chang. If Russia is bent on negotiating a treaty with Corea, the latter should choose an intelligent representative who shall explain to the Russian envoy that she will allow trade on the frontier, but the details will be arranged afterwards. The place fixed on for this trade being so near China, that power should be consulted, and the occasion should be taken for arranging the principal point, which is to settle the question of fugitives by international law, and if you have to carry on the negotiations verbally have them written down. It is doubtful if the Coreans will obtain a satisfactory result, as both modern and ancient history show the injustice of strong powers towards weaker ones. And even if the Coreans derive great benefits from the frontier trade, they will not find them a compensation for the troubles it will cause. What will it be then if Corea derives no benefits! If the Russian mission returns to Europe without having negotiated the treaty, Corea will soon find herself in great trouble.

The treaty ought to be made, but great care is necessary. If your Government disdains this advice, it will soon repent of it. Such are the words I wished to say to you, it is for Your Majesty to see if they are right or not.

297   *Confidential*   23 April 1886

Secretary of State

Sir:

I have to report that O. N. Denny Esq. has been commissioned by His Majesty the King of Korea as Vice President of the Home Office and Director of Foreign Affairs in the Foreign Office. Through the position in the Home Office, Judge Denny becomes the direct Advisor of His Majesty.

In my despatch No. 290 I referred to the opposition then being made to Judge Denny's entry into the service of Korea by Mr. Yuan, the Chinese representative here. This opposition was of a very marked character and excited the deep interest of all the foreign representatives here, who were favorable to Judge Denny's being placed in a position of accessibility to the King. Mr. Yuan, after using every endeavor to have Judge Denny made simply an Advisor in the Foreign Office, where it was intended he should serve with a Chinese official, by operating on the Foreign (Office) officers and individual nobles of high authority, finally had audience with his Majesty and advised directly Judge Denny's being placed in the Foreign Office simply. His Majesty, doubtless strengthened by the support given to Judge Denny by the other foreign representatives, replied that the status of Judge Denny would be decided upon by his own Ministers of State.

On the following morning, the commission appointing him to office in both the Foreign Office and Home Offices was issued. At one time the opposition of Mr. Yuan took the form of intimidation of certain officers detailed to attend Judge Denny by His Majesty and in order to check it, Judge Denny telegraphed to request action of the Viceroy Li Chung Fang. Notwithstanding the facts as I have reported to the Department, there has appeared under Tientsin correspondence in one of the China newspapers a paragraph to the effect that the King of Korea refused to receive Judge Denny until he was compelled to do so through a telegraphic despatch from the Viceroy, handed him by Mr. Yuan.

There can be no doubt but that the violent and pretentious attitude shown by Mr. Yuan has only tended to draw adherents toward His Majesty and to weaken considerably Mr. Yuan's influence on all sides. It is not possible to ascertain with certainty whether Mr. Yuan is acting solely under the instructions of his Government, but the evidences point strongly to such a conclusion.

Our Minister at Peking, Mr. Denby, has informed me of a move of the Viceroy to have Korea included in the mission to Peking. I observe that this move was coincident with Mr. Yuan's announcing himself as "resident" in Söul. I was recently informed at his office that two of Mr. Yuan's assistants bore the rank of Vice President of the Korean Foreign Office; also that another assistant was proposed to serve with him as Secretary for Foreign Affairs. At the same time, Mr. Yuan to the Government of Korea represents himself simply as Minister.

The Customs of Korea would appear to have been incorporated in the Customs of China, the most direct evidence of this being that the Customs Trade Reports—a copy of which I have already transmitted to the Department—appear as a section merely of the General Report of the Chinese Customs—in the same manner as though Korea were but a province of China.

From such facts as I have herein cited it seems to me that China now aims at something at least akin to incorporation of Korea into her own empire. If such a move be intended, it comes too late and must fail. At present China is greatly weakened in adherents to her policy here among Koreans, while Koreans are more than usually united in guarding the independence they possess practically, and are greatly strengthened by the treaties with Western Powers. The country is quiet, and fresh signs of progress are visible among the people. It is reasonable to predict a period of progress and general improvement of the Kingdom in the near future.

George C. Foulk

NO. 3.
Secretary of State

Legation of the United States
Söul, Korea
September 8, 1886

Sir:

I have the honor to submit the following relating to the recent political disturbance in Söul, which formed the subject of Mr. Parker's despatch, from this legation, No. 26, Diplomatic Series, dated August 25th, ultimo. My information is based upon the remarks of the several representatives in Söul, verbal accounts from Koreans who were concerned in the affair, letters received by me at Nagasaki from Korean officials and Dr. H. N. Allen, and observation made by me prior to my leaving Korea in July last.

In June, last Judge Denny, in his capacity of Adviser to the Korean Government, began to assist the government in a correspondence with the English Government aimed to effect the release of Port Hamilton from the military occupation being maintained by the latter government. England had represented that the occupation was but temporary, (and unavoidable owing to the fact that Korea was not in a position to prevent the Port Hamilton group from falling into the hands of a power (Russia) between which and England relations were strained. In its later protests against the occupation, Korea had shown with apparently much precision and force that the grounds on which England had made the occupation no longer existed. In reply to these later protests, Korea recently received answers favorable to the raising of the occupation.

Early in August an article appeared in a native newspaper in Söul, giving the report of a Korean official on the presence of a Russian vessel of war at Port Lazeroff on the East Korean coast. The vessel was described as having three masts. By a mistranslation of this article, Mr. Baber, Consul General of England in Söul, understood the report to refer to the presence of a fleet of four Russian vessels at Port Lazareff, and informally brought his knowledge of the presence of such a fleet to the attention of Mr. Waeber, Chargé D'Affaires of Russia in Söul. Mr. Waeber stated he was ignorant of the presence of the fleet at Port Lazareff and examined the article in the newspaper himself, finding it referred to but one Russian man-of-war, a surveying vessel, of whose movements he was well aware; he called the attention of Mr. Baber to his mistranslation some days later.

Confidential

Mr. Waeber has told me that he believes Mr. Baber telegraphed the presence of a Russian fleet at Port Lazareff to Peking, and communicated it to the Chinese representative in Söul, Mr. Yuen Si Kwai, before his error in translating the newspaper article had been discovered.

On or about August 16th, Judge Denny received telegraphic inquiries from the Viceroy Li Hung Chang. He called on the same date upon the Chinese representative, and unexpectedly found him haranging a large number of Korean officials of high rank. The Tai Wön Kun had just left the legation, and chief among the Koreans present was Prince Min Yong Ik (who returned to Korea from China in July last). Mr. Yuen stated that he had accurate knowledge of an agreement in writing, bearing the King's seal, the effect of which was to turn Korea bodily over to Russian protection. He went on to say in a wildly exciting manner that China would at all hazards put an end to such a movement,—would send on his summons 75,000 soldiers into Korea,—that he would die fighting, &c, &c, &c.

Judge Denny asked to see the copy of Agreement bearing the Royal Seal—which Mr. Yuen declared himself possessed of, and strongly insisted upon it that if such a paper existed it was a forgery. He proceeded then to admonish Mr. Yuen upon his rash excitement, pointing out that it tended to create grave disorder in which the lives of foreigners in Söul would be endangered. Mr. Yuen stated that he had been informed from China of the secret intrigues between Korea and Russia, and chided by the Viceroy for his ignorance of what was going on in Korea. Judge Denny then vigorously charged Mr. Yuen with being the sole author of any such information as had reached China; that instead of China's discovering the so-called agreement, Mr. Yuen had invented it and telegraphed his erroneous assumptions to China.

Mr. Yuen had already been to the Palace. His manner there had been

Struggle for Control

violently excited. He threatened to call to Korea a Chinese army. He later said himself to Judge Denny, that at one time while he was in the presence of the King, he thought blows would be resorted to.

Judge Denny saw Mr. Waeber, who treated the whole matter quietly and lightly, giving his word of honor that he was in ignorance of any agreement or reported agreement concerning the relations of Russia & Korea.

On Saturday, Aug. 13th Min Yong Ik had excitedly appeared before the King to announce that word had come from China saying a Korean official had telegraphed to the Viceroy Li that, "Korea no longer desired the old relations with China" &c.

On Sunday Aug. 14th the foreign representatives learned of the arrest by the Korean Government of four Korean officials: namely,

Kim Hak U, A highly accomplished officer then acting for His Majesty in the purchase of a steamer from the American Trading Co. of Yokahoma. Had also been employed in many other ways by the King in carrying out progressive reforms.

Kim Ka Chin, A bright young officer distinguished in Korean learning who served with Judge Denny as the latter's means of communication with the King.

Cho Chön Tu, The magistrate of Chuk-san, who had been more or less intimate with foreigners and was interested in several progressive schemes.

Chön Yang Muk, A young officer, who was directing for His Majesty the establishment of the schools for which the American teachers had arrived. Had served with me as Interpreter to this Legation, and upon my departure from Korea had been advanced in rank, and been given charge of a number of important subjects for development in the Western Way by His Majesty.

By reason of their knowledge of foreign civilization and other attainments these four men were pre-eminently in favor at the Palace and most employed in the work of the King and Government of Korea with Western foreigners. It is beyond all doubt that they had long been objectionable to the Chinese authorities. In my despatch No. 297, I reported the intimidation practiced by Mr. Yuen upon Judge Denny's assistants; one of these was Kim Ka Chin. Chön Yang Muk has often told me of his sense of danger from the Chinese faction.

He has told me that in audience Mr. Yuen once produced a list of twenty names of Korean Officers who were pre-eminently progressive in their views and workers of the King, and proposed their removal from office as a means of improving the Government.

Shortly after the arrest of these four officials it was reported they were sentenced to death. Judge Denny and Mr. Kempermann, the German Consul General, separately went to Mr. Yuen and insisted on their release and implied that he was the cause of their apprehension.

Our minister was confined to his bed and incapable; the Russian and English representatives were not in a position to interfere. The real sentence of the four men was that they were worthy of execution, but in lieu of it, were to be banished. This sentence was later revoked and a new one,—to banishment simply was assigned. They were finally released with their offices taken from them.

Kim Hak U has fled the city; the other three are apparently free from danger and quietly residing in Söul.

The charge against the four Koreans was a vague one,—of having interfered in matters of government not pertaining to their offices in speech and action, but it seems to have been understood that the real charge was complicity in the framing of the agreement between Korea and Russia.

The events above described reached the people in distorted accounts, and the report was spread that China had attempted to remove the King and Queen; however, I can learn of no indications or threats of violence among the people. Mr. Yuen's threats and his well-known disposition to do childishly rash things caused the foreigners in Söul some apprehension. Judge Denny and Mr. H. F. Merrill, Commissioner of Customs, approached Minister Parker to suggest his calling a vessel of war to Chemulpho. The "Ossipee" was summoned by a letter dated August 18th. She had been stationed at Chemulpho, but removed temporarily to Chefu on account of cholera at the former place. The telegraph line was reported to be obstructed, though it is commonly said here the line was only reserved for Mr. Yuen's exclusive use.

Judge Denny, to whom duplicity on the part of China in her treatment of Korea must have been suggested by the conduct of Mr. Yuen, had given it out that he should at once proceed to Tientsin to lay Mr. Yuen's conducts before the Viceroy Li. On the 20th instant, Min Yong Ik abruptly sailed for China in a Chinese gunboat, presumably as the agent of Mr. Yuen. His departure from Korea was telegraphed to the Viceroy by Mr. Yuen, who has since learned that Min Yong Ik left the gunboat at Chefoo without explanation: his whereabouts is unknown, and presumably confused and fearful for his life, he has broken off connection with the confused state of affairs of his country and is hiding.

Struggle for Control

The "Ossipee" arrived at Chemulpho on the 24th ultimo. On the 26th Comdr. McGlensey of the "Ossipee" with a force of 20 marines, came to the legation. Copies of correspondence between the Korean Foreign Office and this legation on the subject of the coming of the Marines to Söul, I enclose. The marines were sent back to Chemulpho on August 28th, Captain McGlensey and Assistant Surgeon Russell of the "Ossipee" remaining at the legation; these two officers were summoned to their vessel by Admiral Davis on the day of my arrival in Söul, Sept. 1st.

Judge Denny sailed for Tientsin on a Japanese steamer on Sept. 4th. I had a visit from him before his departure. He goes to see the Viceroy Li to represent the urgent necessity for the removal of Mr. Yuen from his office here, and probably to ascertain clearly his own status in Korea. Mr. Yuen endeavored to proceed to Tientsin at the same time but was ordered to remain at his post by the Viceroy. I now learn that an official of the Korean Foreign Office is to be sent to Tientsin by His Majesty. Undoubtedly, this official is to be the opponent of Judge Denny to oppose Mr. Yuen's removal. I learn confidentially that the Tai Wön Kun, who fears for his life at the hands of the Queen's faction, and regards Mr. Yuen as his protector, has caused the idea to reach His Majesty, that in case Mr. Yuen is removed, disturbances of a serious character may break out amoung the people; it is however probable that the effects of this threat for such it must be on the government, is at the bottom of an officer's being sent to Tient-sin to work for Mr. Yuen, rather than the effect of it on His Majesty.

While during this disturbance there were neither violence nor bloodshed, the effects of it is shown in a great weakening of the King's party. The people are quiet, however, uncertainty and a degree of apprehension being confined to the official classes.

It has long seemed to me that China would make some bold step with the view of suppressing the independent actions of the King of Korea, and placing the country in a position to preclude the obstructions to her complete direction of its affairs. I believe that such a move was meant to be effected during this summer. It was suggested by the presence of a large Chinese fleet moving along the East Coast of Korea from Vladivostock and later visiting Japan—at Nagasaki where it may have been designed to serve as a demonstration against Japanese interference in the move to be made in Korea. The fleet comprised the best war ships of China, and during its stay, pompous efforts were made to show it off to best advantage. A mutiny at Possiette had called certain Russian vessels of war there from Vladivostok. It was the rainy season in Korea, when official activity is at a half-standstill and great quiet prevails among the people. There was a long interval about the middle of August when there was no mail communication with Japan. The opportunity seemed complete, when I learned at Nagasaki that telegraphic communication had been cut off from Söul by inundation in North China.

The move of China became complicated through the actions of the English Consul General in Söul, who some supposed interested himself to secure Port Hamilton anew for England; it is possible also that a very serious conflict between Chinese sailors of the fleet at Nagasaki and the Japanese people there on August 15th checked China from proceeding at full length.

It is evident that the result aimed at by the promoters of the disturbance had not yet been obtained. The results will doubtlessly soon be heard of from Tientsin.

With regard to the presence of the Marines of the "Ossipee" in Söul and my remarks in despatch No. 1, I beg to state that I have only to-day discovered the original letter addressed Minister Parker on the subject by the Korean Foreign Office. I find the translation made for Mr. Parker, and on which he acted, to be incorrect.

Admiral Davis in the "Marion" sailed for Chefoo from Chemulpho on Sept. 6th. I learn that the "Omaha" now at Hakodate, will be sent to Chemulpho at an early date.

George C. Foulk

NO. 13.   October 14, 1886

Confidential

Secretary of State

Sir:

With reference to my despatch No. 3, dated September 8th ultimo, having for its subject the political disturbance in Söul of August last, I have now to report that Judge Denny has returned to Korea from Tientsin and has communicated to me at some length the substance of his interviews with the Viceroy Li Chung Fang. The information I have thus obtained is fully in harmony with the opinions expressed in my despatch—that the disturbance in Söul was created by the Chinese representative here in an attempt of China to suppress the independent sovereignty of this Kingdom, and that the attempt was frustrated by unexpected complications in Söul

Struggle for Control 155

and the fight between sailors of the Chinese fleet at Nagasaki and the police and people at that place.

Judge Denny reports that in his earlier interviews, the Viceroy was disposed to defend the Chinese representative here—Mr. Yuan—against the charges vigorously brought against him by Judge Denny and Mr. H. F. Merrill, the American Chief Commissioner of Korean Customs. The chief charge was that Mr. Yuan had created copies of a purported agreement bearing the seal of the King of Korea by which Korea was turned into a protectorate of Russia; assuming that the announced existance of these copies would create the impression that a real agreement had been made, he believed that China's right to absorb Korea would be established. These copies were, however, denounced as forgeries from the beginning by Judge Denny, Mr. Merrill, and the several foreign representatives except the Consul General of England, and the two officers named brought these opinions to the attention of the Viceroy by telegrams and letters. The Viceroy and Peking government thus discovered that their ruse was detected; thus with the affair at Nagasaki, which foreboded difficulty with Japan, checked effectually the move intended.

Judge Denny states that while the Viceroy is charged with the control of Korean affairs for China, it was not at his original instance that Mr. Yuan made the attempt in Söul; that the scheme originated in the Peking government, which ordered the Viceroy to furnish ships of war and men necessary to Mr. Yuan to effect the suppression of Korea. The Viceroy conveyed the idea to Judge Denny that England through her representative at Peking has long been urgently pressing the government there to incorporate Korea into her own Empire out and out. The plan decided upon by China was to remove the King, Queen, and Crown Prince of Korea to China, place the Tai Wön Kun temporarily at the head of affairs in Korea (because of his popularity and power with the people), and finally to create out of her a new province of the Chinese Empire.

Judge Denny states that the Viceroy fully appreciate the inexpediency of the annexation of Korea, and realize that England is operating in relation to Korea, out of purely selfish motives; also that the Peking government has had its eyes opened to the fact that it has been handled as a tool by England at the risk of bringing grave trouble upon China. The English minister had just proposed to China the opening of Port Hamilton and had announced his intention of proceeding to Korea to effect the necessary arrangements. With regard to this, Judge Denny states he endeavored to satisfy the Viceroy with such a mission of the English minister would be useless—that Korea could not entertain the proposition, and that in view of the manner in which England had occupied the Port, Korea could only insist upon its release—and that it was China's plain duty to maintain Korea's stand in the matter. To these remarks the Viceroy gave his approval.

After considerable discussion as to the most feasible in which the inviolability of Korea could be preserved, it was finally decided upon that China should ask Russia to enter into an agreement providing for the neutrality of the Korean Peninsula, as regards to the two nations. The Russian minister at Peking was consulted in this connection by the Viceroy and by Judge Denny. Upon leaving Tientsin, Judge Denny was informed by the Viceroy that Russia had regarded the proposition favorably, and that the agreement would soon be effected.

At Nagasaki, the investigation of the affray there on August 15th by Chinese and Japanese officials, is being prolonged while there are as yet no evidences of a speedy satisfactory settlement. It is apparently the attitude of China which delays the proceedings. Japan evinces marked irritability over the affair, involving consideration of Korea. It is now reported on good authority that Mr. Takahira Kogoro, the present Chargé d'Affaires of Japan to Korea is about to be recalled and the impression is popular that Japan will place in his stead an official prepared to deal more summarily with questions involving Korea and Japan and China. In this connection I may quote from my dispatch No. 306, dated June 2, 1886—"Mr. Takahira impressed to me clearly that the attitude of China has reached a point at which the misunderstanding arrived at in the convention at Tientsin, in regard to Korea, has been departed from, and the interference by his government would seem to be imperatively necessary."

I beg to point out that in the above it is Judge Denny's account and opinion that I have given its relation to the intentions of the Viceroy with respect to Russia and Korea and England. I am not so sanguine that China and Russia will enter into a satisfactory agreement with regard to Korea, though this is to be hoped for, and is desireable to both these governments. England has already a strong hold upon the Peking government and will the more energetical endeavor to create Chinese suspicions of Russia's good faith. I regret to add also, that there is evidence to warrant the belief that Judge Denny has not the support and confidence of the Viceroy;—nor in view of his having been selected and summoned for service in Korea by China, has he the confidence of the progressive or anti-Chinese faction in Korea; thus far he has been permitted no confidential and active part in the affairs of Korea.   George C. Foulk

Index to Documents

1. THE UNITED STATES LEGATION IN SEOUL

NO.	DATE	ORIGINATOR	MAIN SUBJECT	PAGE
1	Mar. 9, 1883	Freylinghuysen	Foote's appointment	23
3	Mar. 17, 1883	Freylinghuysen	Instructions regarding purpose and conduct of Korean-American relations	24
11	June 30, 1883	Foote	Regulation of trade	30
15	Aug. 17, 1883	Adee	Approval of Seoul as legation site	30
17	July 19, 1883	Foote	Advice to King of Korea	31
21	Sept. 18, 1883	Freylinghuysen	Instructions to Foote	31
17	Aug. 17, 1883	Adee	Instructions to Foote	32
27	Oct. 16, 1883	Freylinghuysen	Activities of Korean mission to U.S.	32
28	Oct. 23, 1883	Freylinghuysen	Religious toleration	35
34	Oct. 23, 1883	Foote	U.S. trade in Korea	35
58	July 14, 1884	Freylinghuysen	Reduction in grade of U.S. representative to Korea	36
112	Sept. 17, 1884	Foote	Foote resigns his post	37
10	Nov. 5, 1884	Freylinghuysen	Acceptance of Foote's resignation	38
244	Oct. 20, 1885	Foulk	Legation conditions	38
85	Jan. 18, 1886	Porter	U.S. private interests in Korea	39
279	Feb. 18, 1886	Foulk	Foulk submits his resignation	40
1	Sept. 2, 1886	Foulk	Foulk returns as chargé of the Legation	41
2	Sept. 7, 1886	Foulk	Details on the relief of Minister Parker	42
58	July 31, 1885	Bayard	History of the "General Sherman" case with claims	45

2. SECURING AMERICAN ADVISERS FOR THE KOREAN GOVERNMENT

NO.	DATE	ORIGINATOR	MAIN SUBJECT	PAGE
32	Oct. 19, 1883	Foote	Request of the King for advisers	53
105	Sept. 3, 1884	Foote	Action desired on year-old request	54
109	Sept. 10, 1884	Foote	Request for teachers	55
110	Sept. 17, 1884	Foote	King desires Shufeldt in Korea	56
124	Nov. 15, 1884	Foote	King's patience exhausted	56
14	Nov. 6, 1884	Freylinghuysen	Original request for advisers "mislaid"	57
171	May 15, 1885	Foulk	Result of noncompliance with King's requests	57
184	June 18, 1885	Foulk	Renewed requests for advisers	58
204	July 22, 1885	Foulk	Korean Foreign Office on need for Americans	60
257	Dec. 1, 1885	Foulk	Promises of State Department to send advisers	61
9	Oct. 3, 1886	Foulk	U.S. military advisers needed to forestall Russians	62
10	Oct. 6, 1886	Foulk	Efforts of other powers to supply advisers	63
63	Aug. 19, 1885	Bayard	U.S. position on sending military advisers to Korea	64

Index

3. ENGLAND, RUSSIA, AND KOREA

NO.	DATE	ORIGINATOR	MAIN SUBJECT	PAGE
7	May 1, 1883	Freylinghuysen	News from Peking on Russo-Korean treaty	69
11	June 29, 1883	Davis	News from Tokyo on British refusal to ratify treaty with Korea	70
23	Aug. 21, 1883	Foote	Anglo-Korean treaty	71
37	Oct. 30, 1883	Foote	Anglo-Korean treaty	72
66	April 26, 1884	Foote	Korean desire to modify English treaty	73
172	May 19, 1885	Foulk	Seizure of Port Hamilton	73
174	May 25, 1885	Foulk	England in Port Hamilton	76
180	June 16, 1885	Foulk	Russian attitude on Port Hamilton	77
59	Aug. 18, 1885	Bayard	Instructions to Foulk	78
187	June 26, 1885	Foulk	English attitude on Port Hamilton	78
188	June 26, 1885	Foulk	Arrival of Russian Ambassador	79
189	June 29, 1885	Foulk	Korea requests good offices of the U.S.	79
191	July 3, 1885	Foulk	Russian agent in Korea	80
192	July 5, 1885	Foulk	The Russian position in Korea	81
196	July 6, 1885	Foulk	Korea withdraws request for U.S. mediation	83
223	Sept. 1, 1885	Foulk	English position in Korea	84
238	Oct. 14, 1885	Foulk	Russian requests for trading posts	85
272	Jan. 18, 1886	Foulk	England, Russia, and China in Korea	87
24	Aug. 4, 1886	Parker	Russia and Port Lazareff	89
6	Sept. 24, 1886	Foulk	Proposed Russo-Korean treaty	90

4. CHINA, JAPAN, AND THE STRUGGLE FOR CONTROL OF KOREA

NO.	DATE	ORIGINATOR	MAIN SUBJECT	PAGE
18	July 19, 1883	Foote	Probable return of the ex-Regent	95
104	Sept. 2, 1884	Foote	Chinese troops in Korea	95
127	Dec. 5, 1884	Foote	⎧ The revolt of	96
128	Dec. 17, 1884	Foote and Foulk	⎪ December, 1884,	97
131	Dec. 19, 1884	Foote	⎨ and the situation	113
135	Dec. 29, 1884	Foote	⎩ in Korea	114
136	Dec. 31, 1884	Foote	Arrival of Japanese Special Ambassador	114
137	Jan. 1, 1885	Foote	Arrival of Japanese troops	115
138	Jan. 2, 1885	Foote	Japanese attitude on a settlement	115
139	Jan. 4, 1885	Foote	Chinese attitude on a settlement	116
146	Jan. 31, 1885	Foote	Conservative faction controls Korea	116
177	May 30, 1885	Foulk	Political situation in Korea	118
199	July 10, 1885	Foulk	Chinese and Japanese troops withdraw	119
211	Aug. 4, 1885	Foulk	Activities of Von Möllendorf	120
212	Aug. 6, 1885	Foulk	Contracts with the Korean government	123
70	Sept. 22, 1885	Porter	U.S. policy not to intervene	124
214	Aug. 16, 1885	Foulk	Political situation in Korea	125
215	Aug. 17, 1885	Foulk	Reassertion of Chinese control	127
59	Aug. 18, 1885	Bayard	Position of U.S. vis-à-vis China and Japan in Korea	129
224	Sept. 2, 1885	Foulk	Arms for Korean army	130
231	Sept. 25, 1885	Foulk	Seoul-Peking telegraph	131
237	Oct. 14, 1885	Foulk	Return of the ex-Regent	133
240	Oct. 15, 1885	Foulk	Arrival of Yuan Shi Kai as Chinese Commissioner	135
243	Oct. 20, 1885	Foulk	Interview with the ex-Regent	135
255	Nov. 25, 1885	Foulk	Position of Yuan Shi Kai in Korea	137
260	Dec. 9, 1885	Foulk	Arrival of Denny	140
265	Dec. 29, 1885	Foulk	Rumored invasion of Korea	141

Index

NO.	DATE	ORIGINATOR	MAIN SUBJECT	PAGE
26	Aug. 25, 1886	Parker	Chinese intervention in Korea	144
31	Aug. 18, 1886	Bayard	Li Hung Chang on proposed Russo-Korean treaty	145
297	April 23, 1886	Foulk	Tightened Chinese grip on Korea	147
3	Sept. 8, 1886	Foulk	Chinese intervention in Korea	149
13	Oct. 14, 1886	Foulk	China in control of Korea	154

www.ingramcontent.com/pod-product-compliance
Lightning Source LLC
Chambersburg PA
CBHW021710230426
43668CB00008B/788